THE STUDENT

A Short History

Michael S. Roth

For Irma,

Yale
UNIVERSITY PRESS
NEW HAVEN & LONDON

Published with assistance from the foundation established in
memory of Calvin Chapin of the Class of 1788, Yale College.

Yale University Press books may be purchased in quantity
for educational, business, or promotional use. For information, please e-mail
sales.press@yale.edu (U.S. office) or sales@yaleup.co.uk (U.K. office).

Set in Yale and Alternate Gothic No2 types by IDS Infotech Ltd.
Printed in the United States of America.

Library of Congress Control Number: 2023901275
ISBN 978-0-300-25003-9 (hardcover : alk. paper)

A catalogue record for this book is available from the British Library.

This paper meets the requirements of ANSI/NISO Z39.48-1992
(Permanence of Paper).

10 9 8 7 6 5 4 3 2 1

For Charles Salas

CONTENTS

PREFACE

I've been a teacher and a student for a long time. In high school I tutored children, and in the summers I worked as a swimming instructor. That was in the early 1970s. I began teaching undergraduates when I was pursuing my PhD in history. How thrilling that was! Overflowing with energy, I'd scamper off to the previously off-limits faculty lounge, ready to talk turkey about teaching. It was usually slim pickings. No doubt the more experienced teachers reserved their enthusiasm for the classroom. Were they surprised by mine? I was. I was surprised to discover just how much I enjoyed sitting in the professor's seat. I'd already recognized how much I loved being a student but wasn't sure that would translate to being, so to speak, on the other side of the equation. For an equation of sorts it is. Good students make teachers better, and a great teacher can motivate learning in ways that surpass expectations, including expectations students have of themselves. As a student, I was the nerdy kid who was eager to learn — and perhaps eager to please the teacher, especially in college (at Wesleyan University), when it became clear to me that strong teachers are pleased by being challenged. I have always liked being a student. Even as an instructor, I found ways to stay in a student role — to sit in on lectures, audit seminars, ask questions of colleagues. At my first academic job at Scripps

College, I created a Humanities Institute where fellow professors and advanced undergrads in the humanities could learn from one another and from invited luminaries. It was, I see now, a way for me to remain on the student side of the equation. Years later, I took a job running the Scholars Program at the Getty Research Institute. Noted researchers and artists came from around the world to Los Angeles to work on a problem chosen because my colleagues and I thought it was interesting and open-ended. Although I "led" our weekly seminars, I felt the same sense of intellectual adventure I did as an undergraduate at Wesleyan. At the Getty, too, I got to be on both sides of the equation. I was even able to remain a student when I became a college president in 2000 at the California College of the Arts (then the California College of Arts and Crafts). Since I'm not an artist, I made no bones about the fact that I needed to learn from my colleagues and my students. And their generosity in accepting me as their student was almost as inspirational as their creativity in making their own work.

In 2007 I returned as president to Wesleyan, where I continue to teach and do my best to remain a student. Although coming back to an elite New England liberal arts institution from a California arts school reminded me about the persistence of traditional academic hierarchies, I found that the best way to remain open to learning is the same for a president as it is for a freshman. Acknowledging one's ignorance is the key. And at Wesleyan, there are plenty of people to help me with that!

I have had the good fortune of working with students whose seriousness and joy, playfulness and purpose have illuminated for me powerful works of philosophy, literature, history, and film. In addition to wrestling with, say, Rousseau's *Second Discourse,* Woolf's *To the Lighthouse,* or Sturges's *The Lady Eve,* we have had the experience of thinking for ourselves in amiable company. That experience, I suggest in this book, teaches us something about agency and entanglement and ultimately about freedom. The best teaching invites one to remain a student, someone who stays open to learning, discovery, and even transformation.

There are many people I'd like to thank for contributing to this project. I begin with my creative and thoughtful editor at Yale University Press, Jennifer Banks. Jennifer suggested this general topic to me several years ago, and she has been supportive of my efforts to take a historical approach that aims to illuminate contemporary issues. The whole team at Yale has been wonderful to work with, and I'm especially grateful to Robin DuBlanc for her editorial suggestions. I'd also like to thank my agent, the great Georges Borchardt, who has told me on more than one occasion that he so enjoys his job because it allows him to be a perpetual student. Georges's confidence in my writing has now led to three books at the intersection of culture, politics, history, and education. I owe so much to my own students, who have challenged me over the years because they are so hungry to learn for themselves. At Scripps College and the Claremont Graduate University, at California College of the Arts and Wesleyan University, the people I've had in my classes and tutorials have helped me to continue to learn from old works and have introduced me to cultural productions I would have been unlikely to find on my own. Colleagues at these institutions have been helpful, too, and I'd like especially to thank the President's Office team, Heather Brooke, Dina Burghardt, Anne Laskowski, and Lisa Prokop, for helping me carve out the time to work on this project. My faculty colleagues have offered helpful suggestions: Steve Stemler and Anna

Shusterman in Wesleyan's College of Education Studies, Natasha Korda of the English department, Khalil Anthony Johnson of African American studies, Stephen Angle in philosophy, and Andrew Curran of our French department. The two anonymous referees from the press also made helpful recommendations.

I'm a lucky student of Kari Weil's, who is also my colleague and my wife. She has helped me think more rigorously and creatively about agency and learning, about the fictions of autonomy, and about the pleasures (and responsibilities) of entanglement. I've written most of this book while sitting a short distance from her and can't imagine a better place to be.

For more than thirty years, I have had the great benefits of receiving feedback on my thinking, teaching, and especially my writing from Charles Salas. Charles worked with me as a graduate student in Claremont and as my colleague at the Getty Research Institute and at Wesleyan. We have been friends and students of one another for a long time. Ever since we began studying together, I have learned essential things from him, and it is to him this book is dedicated.

THE STUDENT

INTRODUCTION

There are many ways be a student. Experienced teachers know it's hazardous to generalize about them and so take different approaches depending on who is in the classroom. An approach that works well for one may reduce another to tears. Some students are so eager to please the teacher that they overachieve — finding themselves capable of mastering a subject more quickly than they or their instructor thought possible. Some will strive to find balance and harmony by fitting in to their educational context. Others build intellectual muscle by criticizing every move the teacher makes. By being critical and competitive interlocutors with their instructors, they work harder and learn to think more deeply. Some students learn through imitation, eager to follow their classmates as well as their teacher. There are many ways to be a student, but at their core, this book argues, is developing the capacity to think for oneself by learning from others. The student learns to be more free.

The Student is a short book that takes on a long history, exploring some of the principal models for learning that have developed in very different contexts, from the sixth century BCE to the present.

1

Earlier time periods are painted with very broad strokes; the picture becomes more detailed as we come to the eighteenth-century Enlightenment, when the ideals of freedom and the student become intertwined. Although much ground is covered, I trust it is clear that I make no attempt at being comprehensive. For example, I do not treat the traditions of study in either the Jewish or Muslim traditions, both of which had vital roles in the West. Much of the second half of the book is about American college students, long the subject of commentary and complaint. These days they're accused of being censorious, illiberal, and careerist. There is a long, cliché-ridden history of accusing the young of failing to live up to the older generation's idea of the student. Medieval monks complained about rambunctious priests in training; in the 1960s musical *Bye Bye Birdie* the parents sing, "What's the matter with kids today?" and "Why can't they be like we were, perfect in every way?" This book charts the emergence of the ideal of the student and the inevitable complaints about those who fail to live up to that ideal. We explore concerns of how one should learn from others to develop purpose and agency — noting along the way how actual students learn.

We begin by looking at three ways of being a student: the follower, the interlocutor, and the disciple. Students of Confucius are our starting point, grown men who follow a master in order to learn. For them, learning is linked primarily to living virtuously and harmoniously in relationship with others. We focus on three — each quite different — types of those who pursue an education, types still recognizable in schools today. Next we turn to the students of Socrates, one of the most influential educators in the West. Although the father of Western philosophy cultivated an audience through questioning, he offered no doctrine to which listeners could commit. His students were interlocutors, and they aimed at living an examined life. The self-awareness they practiced would be deemed essential for modern ideas of learning as a path to freedom. Finally, we explore the student as disciple. Jesus's disciples often referred to him as their teacher (or rabbi), and his lessons so profoundly affected them that they felt reborn. They would say they never felt more free than when they walked with Jesus. Discipleship, of course, can still be found in communities of learning.

Aspects of these teachings from long ago live on in all levels of education. Reverence and respect — essential to Confucian practice — are qualities still honored by schools today, although that honoring is often tempered by critique, the mainstay of the Socratic tradition. The spirit of critique (or of critical thinking) to which many university teachers claim fidelity sits uneasily with the faithfulness to tradition that Confucius discussed with his students. Disciples of Jesus show a kind of piety that is even further from Socratic irony, though elements of critique have certainly been useful as they encouraged others to reject the status quo, leave their lives behind, and be born again. For the student of Jesus, imitation of the master is key and understanding is tied to an openness to the love that comes from a community of believers. The invitation to community remains attractive on college campuses, many of which have administrators whose jobs it is to amplify inclusion. The tendency to identify with other true believers, though, is also the dimension of modern student culture that arouses the most pointed criticism. Readers may well recognize aspects of themselves in one or more of these exemplary students from millennia ago.

Next we jump forward, widening our focus to look at what it was like to be "a person with much to learn" in premodern Europe. A person, though not quite a grownup. Someone who needs to understand more about the world in order to operate independently in it.

———

Schools were few and far between during this period, but there was learning nonetheless — learning that aimed at freedom as independence. This was different for boys and girls, to be sure, and gender differences were reflected in formal systems of training such as apprenticeships. Universities were founded in the medieval period, and as literacy became more culturally and economically advantageous, basic schooling became less of an exception. Some people, however, existed outside the realm of learning altogether — at least the kind of learning meant to make one independent. We briefly explore how the category of the slave throws into relief this book's central concern: the link between being a student and freedom. Defenders of slavery had to deny even the possibility that slaves could be students.

At the center of the book (and its central argument) is Kant's late eighteenth-century definition of enlightenment as freedom from self-imposed immaturity. This is the clarion call in the development of the modern idea of the student: someone in the process of learning to think for oneself. Of course, the cultural movement of the Enlightenment was about more than students; it was a process through which many societies strove to liberate themselves from a dependence on tradition and instead use rational thinking to reduce suffering. Science and technology were becoming more useful to a broader sector of the population, and these people required schooling. As a result, more and more families in the eighteenth century were becoming familiar with the idea of the student. Theories of education were hotly debated, and over time those debates came to have less to do with faith and salvation, focusing instead on preparing independent thinkers who could also be free citizens. These debates grow only more complex in the nineteenth century, as formal schooling becomes widespread in the West. Are schools truly helping students think for themselves, or are they only indoctrinating them into the latest conventions? Will advanced learning lead to scientific gains that benefit society, or will it only create self-serving justifications for the inequalities associated with the increased pace of industrialization? If everyone is learning the same thing, how can one speak about learning to think for oneself? We end this section of the book with Ralph Waldo Emerson's bracing call to live more independently by being more open and creative. Real students, Emerson taught, are provoked away from conformity. Freedom, for Emerson, was not just an intellectual matter. It was bound up with living with an intensity opposed to convention.

The life of W.E.B. Du Bois gives us an anomalous but powerful lens through which to examine changes in what it meant to be a student. Du Bois's educational experiences were extraordinarily diverse — from his childhood schooling in Western Massachusetts to his undergraduate years at a school for black students in the South to his studies at distinguished universities in America and abroad with some of the greatest minds of the day. Du Bois pursued his own education with a steeliness forged by racist opposition to his talents and ambitions. As a student, he aimed at freedom through empowerment. During his lifetime higher education expanded dramatically, as greater numbers of people came to see a college diploma as a promise of future independence or of their capacity to contribute to the world around them.

The example of Du Bois leads to further consideration of changes in college education for women and African Americans trying to get ahead in a nation undergoing rapid transformation. We note the appearance of student "types" on campuses — from the "college man" ensconced in his fraternity to the "campus radical" convinced that thinking for oneself means totally rejecting the status quo. Where the former often saw freedom as independence from school authorities, the latter found freedom in a more Emersonian rejection of conformity. We then consider campus protest movements that sometimes see the university as a platform from which to oppose society's injustices – and other times view higher education itself as a symptom of those injustices.

Taking off from the student movement of the 1960s, we arrive at modern-day conceptions of the student. As the Vietnam War ended and student activism waned, some critics bemoaned the shift in student focus toward getting good grades or just getting ahead. They worried that young people were no longer asking questions of meaning and value and instead were seeing their education in instrumentalist terms. How can I use my diploma to get into an even better professional school or to be a more competitive job applicant? But the loudest critique of college students, usually aimed at those few attending elite schools, complained about a different kind of conformity among the young: the conformity of political correctness. Students were said to enforce political conformity with social ostracism while avoiding hard questions about their own (progressive) pieties. With the end of the Cold War, conservative intellectuals looked to campuses to find the enemy within – radicals who were self-righteously committed to changing the world in their own image. Even liberals eventually joined in, unhappy to find themselves the targets of student objections to the way things are. Now the student is said to be censorious or relativist, illiberal or radical, coddled snowflake or warrior for social justice. In recent years, as the bogeyman of political correctness has been transformed in the minds of its enemies into woke and cancel culture, one can see more clearly than ever that the idea of the student is a screen onto which older folks project their anxieties and fears.

—

For decades now, politicians and commentators have worried about whether students exercise or smother freedom of speech, and most recently state legislators have intervened directly in establishing what kinds of history and literature will be taught in schools. Some states have recently passed bills forbidding teachers from discussing "critical race theory," by which they seem to mean any scholarship about anti-black racism that doesn't see it as a wild aberration from the norms of American history. Some of the bills forbid "divisive concepts" that might make a group of people feel uncomfortable or guilty. And then there's the fear that any discussion of the brutalities of racist oppression will undermine the possibilities for patriotism in the future. Researchers at UCLA have found nearly five hundred examples of bills around the country that try to limit teaching about slavery and discrimination.[1]

Although provoked by anti-racist initiatives in the last few years, these efforts to protect supposedly fragile students aren't limited to scholarship about African Americans. Art Spiegelman's graphic memoir *Maus,* which deals with the Holocaust, was banned in 2022 in a Tennessee school district, and there has been a widespread effort in some states to remove from school library shelves any books that deal with LGBTQ issues. At a time of polarization, it is not surprising to find tensions in our society expressed in relation to young people in school—sometimes because we can imagine them as being vulnerable to harm and sometimes because we see their ideas as dangerous.

As technology and education have become more closely entangled, digitally minded educators have sought to escape polarizing debates about students by emphasizing only the acquisition of specific skills. Political debates are more easily bracketed when one is being trained to code or to get a diploma in, say, forensic accounting.

—

Some teachers have dropped the term *students* altogether, preferring to speak of *learners*. Skill development for learners resulting in micro-certificates has often been linked to online education, though gamification and certification can be used in a variety of settings. One might get help from a ProfBot in an online class, but one might also get a digital badge in a traditional university chemistry class because one completed the fun safety-training game. Machine learning is already correcting (and perhaps writing) term papers, and it may turn out to be a model for education as ingestion/digestion – not the most progressive vision. The embrace of educational technology by teachers has already had its share of "be careful what you wish for" moments. Those tech-savvy teachers who advocate for the use of "learners" insist they want classrooms filled with active pupils, not passive recipients of instruction. This emphasis on active learning recalls the language of freedom that has been associated with the idea of the student for centuries, but in our contemporary economy the desire for specific skills certified by a teacher (or bot) speaks more to the desire for efficiency, for repeatable knowledge that can be put to use. Perhaps this is the capitalist version of Confucian harmony: students as learners shown how to productively fit in, how to conform so as to succeed. The diploma – or more likely a badge or certificate – is their signal to employers that they have learned the lessons of conformity well.

But even in our digital era, the idea of the student as a whole person in the process of learning how to be free remains potent. Although people coming of age today surely benefit from developing specific skills for operating in a world of algorithms and machines, we also want them to be able to cultivate practices that enable them to flourish as individuals and members of communities. These practices aim to develop what earlier periods called "virtues" – qualities

---

we still seek in our neighbors, colleagues, and leaders. Confucius, Socrates, and Jesus emphasized in their own ways the importance of these virtues for community, and their teachings invited followers, interlocutors, and disciples to flourish in concert with those around them. Medieval apprentices were expected to learn not just how to practice a trade but also how to belong to their community in mutually beneficial ways. Today when we speak of student character and community, we point to our need for lifelong learners, people whose openness to ambiguity will allow them to navigate in our world with integrity and compassion. We need tech-savvy people, to be sure, but we also need citizens who have been students of the world and who have developed curiosity, judgment, and creativity.

All people have capacities; students are those who set out to discover what theirs might be and then work on developing them. Many around the world are denied this opportunity for multidimensional development. Those who have this opportunity and fail to seize it — those who willfully neglect their capacities and squander chances to fulfill their potential — are, at best, clinging to immaturity. At worst, they are engaging in a form of self-mutilation. The true student embraces possibilities for growth. This flourishing is different from being trained by an instructor to do a task, and it is different from the satisfaction one gets through acquiring objects or experiences in the marketplace. Students do learn specific tasks, and they do enjoy experiences, of course, but *as students* they are doing something more fundamental. They are learning freedom by learning who they are and what they can do (including how they might think). This almost always happens in concert with others. Students flourish by discovering and developing their capacities together.

In the past couple of years, the importance of this flourishing came to the fore as the conditions that support it were taken away.

During the COVID-19 pandemic, many schools were shut down or "went remote." Truncating the experience of being a student was painful for many and may well turn out to have negative long-term consequences. This is not just about learning via the internet. I have taught online classes for years, and I know that many people can learn much on various platforms currently available across a wide variety of fields. Remote education has benefits. But, like many teachers, I found the return to face-to-face classes (even mask-to-mask classes) invigorating. And I was not alone. My students, most of whom are sophisticated at maintaining online relationships with their friends and families, were as energized as I was by being back in the classroom. My colleagues and I were surprised when many students thanked us for teaching as they packed up to leave class. Each week! They weren't thanking us for information we had shared with them. They were expressing gratitude for having the opportunity to build intellectual muscles, to stretch their imaginations. Although there are surely "aha moments" that happen in solitary study or practice, our students were also grateful for learning to-gether—for being in the company of others who, like themselves, were developing their capacities.

In this book we look at students as followers and interlocutors, disciples and rebels, children and young people coming into their own as adults. There is no path that works for everyone, though ac-knowledging one's ignorance is a good start for most. The idea of the student emerges alongside the idea that learning is a process, and even when you are no longer an apprentice or a novice, that process in the best of cases has no terminus. You don't arrive at some final Truth because when it seems you are at the end of one path of inquiry, you just (if you're lucky) realize you are on another. As we come to recognize that all people have multifarious capacities and that these should not be defined in advance of the opportunity for exploring them, that they have the potential for freedom, we see the significance of the student — of the state of exploring how to interact with the world, absorbing its lessons and creatively responding to them.

Why one would ever want to really graduate from this state is beyond me.

Chapter 1

ICONIC TEACHERS, EXEMPLARY STUDENTS

Anyone who wants to learn or to follow a new path has to find the right teacher. But the right teacher can be hard to find. One can seek out a wise person from whom one can absorb lessons about oneself and the world, or someone able to raise doubts about received wisdom, or simply someone whose life is worth emulating. Some teachers are powerful because they attract followers while others are compelling because they prize independence and don't want anyone to walk in their footsteps.

It's also hard for a teacher to find the right students, those with the will and capacities to learn. This has been a perennial quest for those with skills, ideas, or a mission to share. It remains a central question for educational institutions today as they determine how best to devote their resources to serve both the individuals who want to learn and the societies of which they are a part. Some schools and teachers are selective, seeking only those who have already demonstrated that they can do a lot with the resources available to them; others prize access, eager to leave their marks on minds that are blank slates. At various times in Western history, authors have pic-

—

tured students as extraordinarily receptive people – sponges who soak up the lessons they are exposed to. At other times, students are imagined as rebels who have learned how to reject the status quo.

To better understand these conflicting ideas of the student, we begin with models of learning and learners from three of the deepest traditions of education still encountered today. Students have been seen as followers, interlocutors, friends, disciples, and/or beneficiaries, and these images resonate with models of learning and learners from vital pedagogical traditions. Our first group traveled with Confucius as he taught about ritual, legitimacy, and learning to live well in tumultuous times; the second comprised interlocutors of Socrates who absorbed a powerful mode of questioning that would shape the history of philosophy and critical thinking. The third group was composed of apostles. Jesus was their teacher, and they expressed their devotion to his lessons as a commitment to follow the path he set out. Elements of these three models of how to be a student will reappear throughout the history of the West, and in the modern period they will all be situated in relation to conflicting ideas of human freedom.

Confucianism is a philosophical tradition that has for centuries been the foundation of East Asian educational institutions and practices. Scholars have adapted its core tenets in relation to changing political and economic contexts, and sometimes in opposition to the reigning authorities of a given time and place. Today Neo-Confucianism has found adherents among Communist Party officials in China and among advocates for liberalism and social change in Asia and around the world. Kong Fuzi (Kong was the family name, Fuzi an honorific added later and then Latinized in the seventeenth century as

Confucius) lived from 551 to 479 BCE. Son of an impoverished aristocrat who died when Confucius was only three, he grew up in poverty. It's hard to have too much confidence in the historical accuracy of the legends surrounding Confucius's early years, but he is said to have distinguished himself early in life by his commitment to learning. In 540 BCE, there were six arts that well-to-do and aristocratic people were supposed to cultivate: ritual, music, archery, charioteering, calligraphy, and arithmetic. Scholars were also supposed to demonstrate a familiarity with the classical traditions, especially through poetry and song. Mastering these arts meant that one had acquired very specific skills, but it also meant that one had exercised self-discipline – that one was learning to master oneself. Confucius wanted to follow this path.

Confucius's family had fallen from the noble class into a class of "gentlemen," or *shi,* which meant that the young man had connections to traditions of elite culture but lacked the ready means to use those connections to better his situation. Having acquired an education despite his economic status, Confucius set out to develop skills that would make him useful to those with power and influence. His home province of Lu suffered through rounds of political turmoil as elites jockeyed for power. In the aftermath of these struggles, minor princes or warlords turned to members of the shi class, whose basic education and cultural knowledge could be helpful in stabilizing governance and overseeing taxation. Shi could be normalizers, if not the creators of new norms. They could be helpful in finding ways to end the fighting, they could make arguments from history and propose reasonable modes of behavior that would eventually be translated into laws, and they could help in creating legitimacy and stability.

Although Confucius certainly took legitimation through law seriously (at one point working as a bureaucrat), his approach to

---

teaching was not legalistic. Instead, he wanted to find a path for a life well lived as an individual and in relation to one's community, which included traditions and ancestors. Much of his life was devoted to working out an understanding of virtue, harmony, and historical continuity that would be less dependent on family rank and more attuned to the integrity of a person's beliefs and behavior. He took on this project without the protection of rank or military strength, and so he had to pursue it carefully, even modestly.

Before he became a teacher, or "master," Confucius served as minister of crime in the region of Lu. After falling out with those in power, Confucius went into a kind of self-imposed exile. We can't be sure if he was forced to leave his region because he backed the wrong party, or if he left because he was disillusioned with those he had been serving. What is known is that there was unrest in the city of Qi, part of the Lu region. A group of rebellious families had gained control of the city, upsetting traditional lines of authority. The oldest source we have says cryptically: "The men of Qi made a present of singing and dancing girls. The people of Qi made a present of female musicians. Ji Huanzi received them, and for three days he did not attend court. Confucius departed."[1]

Something was amiss in the ritual practices, and Confucius no longer had a civic position. Warring families were competing for control, and the minister of crime may have backed the losing side. A group known as the Three Families was trying to gain control of the region, and one of the master's protégés, Zilu, urged on their rebellion. The result was disastrous for the families and their allies, and perhaps Confucius was implicated in their fall. In any case, he was a teacher of comity and continuity, and in such a volatile political situation it seemed impossible to impose new patterns of legitimacy or to create a consensus among those vying violently for power.

The appropriate relation to tradition had been broken, at least in public life. What we know as Confucianism comes from this period when the master left the realm of civic responsibility. Whether or not he did so voluntarily, Confucius abandoned the world of politics and took to the road with an itinerant band of students.

Sometime in the late 490s BCE, when Confucius was in his fifties, he began his travels and his teaching. He had few traditional responsibilities — his parents were long dead, and his children were grown. Students of Confucius had a simple expectation: to be able to talk with their teacher. The best source we have for those conversations, the one compiled nearest to the time in which they took place, is *The Analects*. This volume is said to have been prepared by Confucius's students and *their* students, and it continued to be revised in the two centuries after the master's death. Conversation with the teacher was described as a vocation and a joy that could be deepened through practice: "To study and at due times practice what one has studied, is this not a pleasure? When friends come from distant places, is this not joy? To remain unsoured when his talents are unrecognized, is this not a *junzi*?"[2] The junzi is a learned gentleman, an individual who has cultivated the Six Arts and has arrived at a balanced life characterized by rectitude and social standing. The fact that one's talent might not be recognized, say, in the political arena, would not "sour" this gentleman. Like Confucius, the junzi would not let failures in the political realm affect how he lived his life, a life in which the practices of study and conversation were central.

In addition to the Six Arts, the junzi sought a general orientation toward the past through *Li*, which can be described as "the rites and rituals that have been passed down in instruction (formal and informal) ranging from political protocol to court ceremony, religious rites to village festivals."[3] One's everyday behavior toward others was considered an aspect of Li. So too was one's conduct when alone.

The main goal of learning and practicing the rituals was the development of one's inherent potential: one's *De*, or virtue. Practices such as the Six Arts cultivate one's De so as to promote a practical wisdom that influences others while being grounded in ethical self-possession. Confucius combined an emphasis on self-cultivation with a relational approach, a social approach, to the self. He saw the realization of individual potential in relation both to those who came before (the temporal context) and to those with whom one interacts in the present (the social context). The realization of De was contagious and thus helped foster harmony in a given community.

Harmony is a central idea for Confucius and the traditions that stem from his teaching. It is through a balance of differences rather than their erasure that one creates a good meal, a good conversation, a good community, a good self. When all of these are balanced through a person's character and interactions, one has developed *Ren*. Ren has been translated in a variety of ways: benevolence, humaneness, goodness. Ren is "the valuable, intelligible way that things fit together," as one commentator on the *Analects* puts it.[4]

As Confucius retreated from the city and his civic responsibilities, he and his followers left behind an environment of disharmony and violence in which relations to the past and to society were in disarray. There was little hope of creating more harmony in the world around them. The group wasn't completely disconnected from the political or civic realm; indeed, their conversations often turned to those topics. But Confucius ceased to be a functionary and became a teacher; through this work he became the founder of a path of education. And *path* is a key word for Confucians, a serviceable translation of *Dao*. The journey of the Dao to Ren is one of continual education as an individual and as a facet of a harmonious collective.

The sources are unreliable about the numbers of followers who wandered with the master — the figures range from dozens to thousands. Zigong, Zilu, and Yan Hui are three followers who came to represent modes of learning and faithful following. In the traditions of Confucianism, these three are models for students and teachers alike.[5]

Zigong is one of the primary interlocutors of Confucius in the *Analects*. Thirty-one years younger than Confucius, he is a successful businessman who has served as a diplomat and political official, and he is concerned with how the master's general pronouncements about a good life can be applied to the exigencies of commerce and politics. Although he is known as one of the most eloquent of the followers, Zigong's limitations are often underscored by his teacher, who reminds him that fine speeches, punctilious action, or imitative practice are not substitutes for reflection and understanding.

As a man of experience in business and politics, Zigong is adept at sizing up other people, and in the tradition he is known as someone who can easily acquire new skills and productively adapt to new situations. But this is also taken to mean that he lacks refinement and the patience to develop into a junzi of deep rectitude and wisdom. It is Zigong's worldly success that spurs him on to more mundane achievements at the expense of truly cultivating his own potential. Although Confucius has more exchanges with the politician/businessman than anyone else, he describes his energetic student as a "vessel," having said earlier that the junzis are not mere vessels.[6] Some believe that this points to Zigong's lack of creativity or initiative, but Confucius also describes him as a very *special* vessel, one that holds offerings in the ancestral temple; "Only with you can one discuss the Odes," the master tells him. Only Zigong, it seems, has deeply understood some of the key teachings found in the most ancient poetry.[7]

Zigong is sometimes faulted by his master for judging people too harshly. The student is chided for being too tough a teacher! "What a worthy man that Zigong must be! As for me, I hardly have the time for this," he remarks when Zigong is being too harsh or nitpicking in his criticisms of others. But Confucius, too, could be direct in his criticism. In one of their most famous exchanges, Zigong says, "What I do not wish others to do to me, I do not wish to do to others." The master replies, "Ah, Zigong! This is a level you have not yet reached."[8] Confucius sees Zigong as the kind of student who seeks to do well with the lessons, to master the material, but who lacks genuine insight and empathy. When Zigong repeats the formula of reciprocity (*Shu*) that one should not do to others what one doesn't want for oneself, his teacher is skeptical that the businessman has really understood what this means as a way of life. It seems that Zigong is the kind of student who knows how to write a good paper, how to get a good grade, but who hasn't developed the inner strength to really live the lessons that he has studied. Confucius encourages and criticizes Zigong by turns — recognizing that his successful, practical student needs to work on expanding his moral imagination.[9] The teacher expects the student to grow, but he doesn't set unreasonable expectations for a person whose striving can take him only so far.

If a weakness of Zigong's was a quickness to judge others, the weakness of Zilu was his quickness to act, to leap into the fray. This follower of Confucius became known for his courage, even his brashness, and his fidelity to the master was second to none. When Zilu asks his teacher, probably with high expectations, whom he would choose to lead armies against his rivals, Confucius replies, "Those who fight tigers with their bare hands, wade across rivers, and are willing to die without regret—I would not want their company. I would certainly want those who approach affairs with fearful caution and who like to lay careful plans for success." Although this was meant to remind Zilu of the work he still had to do to cultivate himself as a moral being, Confucius is fond of this rough-hewn man of action, recognizing that no one is more willing to sacrifice himself for his teacher. Though their conversations often seem harsh, it is a directness born of affection. It is also what this particular student needs in order to learn. This teacher calibrates his lessons according to the student's needs—sometimes pushing them forward, sometimes holding them back. At a moment of disappointment with the immoral world around him, Confucius declares, "The *dao* does not prevail! I shall set out over the sea on a raft. I expect that Yóu [Zilu] will be willing to accompany me." One can imagine Zilu's pleasure in hearing the master single out his fidelity, but his teacher quickly complicates the picture, saying his student's "love of valor exceeds mine; there is nowhere to get the lumber," meaning, But where am I to find really suitable material?[10] Commentators take him to be making a joke at Zilu's expense—Zilu may be loyal and brave but that is not enough. Courage, we learn in the *Analects*, must be combined with practice in order to develop Ren, to move along the Way.

Confucius fears that his student's recklessness will get him killed one day—and it does. Reversing his master's steps, Zilu goes from self-cultivation to working in the political sphere, becoming a magistrate in the town of Wey. During an insurrection there, Zilu is killed in a valiant but ill-advised attempt to rescue his prince.

Zilu was the type of student who needed criticism, and Confucius delivered it. When a talented student is also headstrong, the teacher tries to modify or redirect the aggressive energies in ways that will prove more educative than dangerous. Hearing the critiques, other followers imagined themselves superior to their hotheaded compatriot, and the master found ways to correct them, too. Zilu had not reached the goal, but he was determined to make progress; he was on his way. He revered his teacher, and his teacher was in turn grateful for his loyalty. Such devotion wasn't the same as wisdom or benevolence, but it was an important dimension of a student's harmonious existence. Confucius wanted Zilu and the other followers to understand that virtuous qualities would lead to Ren and living as a junzi only if they were combined with self-cultivation and learning: "If you love ren, but you do not love learning, the flaw is ignorance. If you love knowledge but you do not love learning, the flaw is unruliness. If you love faithfulness but you do not love learning, the flaw is harming others. If you love straightforwardness but you do not love learning, the flaw is offensiveness. If you love valor but you do not love learning, the flaw is causing chaos. If you love incorruptibility but you do not love learning, the flaw is recklessness."[11] Here Confucius is pointing out that loving learning means always being open to changing course, or at least finding ways to modify one's trajectory. Pursuing a good can lead to bad outcomes if the pursuit is undertaken with arrogance or certainty, if it isn't leavened with the love of learning that comes with being a student.

If Zigong is skillful in commerce and Zilu in war, Yan Hui is the student whose devotion to learning most impressed the teacher: "There was Yan Hui who loved learning. He never shifted his anger, never repeated his errors. Unfortunately, his life was short and he died. Now there is none." Roughly thirty years younger than the master, Yan Hui is often described as his favorite student. When his teacher is critical, it is because he wonders whether Yan Hui is himself being critical enough — if the young man is too much the disciple. "Yan Hui is no help to me at all: he delights in anything I say." But more often the teacher marvels at how much his young protégé can absorb and never tire of contemplating the Way. Hui is quiet during their exchanges and doesn't argue with his teacher. At first Confucius wonders what the young man has learned. "But when I observe how he behaves in private after he's retired from my presence, I can see that he's learned everything I've taught him. Indeed, Hui isn't slow at all."[12] The strong student absorbs lessons, taking them to heart.

Yan Hui seems physically fragile, and Confucius expresses worry about his student's well-being. Although Yan Hui jokes that he would not dare die while the master is still alive, the young man does indeed pass away. Confucius is overcome with grief, crying out, "Heaven is destroying me!" His followers said, "You have wailed beyond proper bounds, Master," criticizing the teacher for "excessive mourning." But Confucius responds: "If I do not wail beyond proper bounds for this man, then for whom?" The affection between student and teacher ran deep.[13]

Yan Hui's pure love of learning clearly inspired Confucius, as great students often inspire their teachers. The young man did not aim at either possessions or victory, unlike Zigong and Zilu. Yan Hui recognized that one never possesses learning the way one possesses the gains of commerce or war. He had "neared perfection" but still lived in poverty, and he understood that learning as self-cultivation, the Way, was a never-ending process: "With a great sigh Yan Hui lamented, 'The more I look up at it the higher it seems; the more I delve into it, the harder it becomes. Catching a glimpse of it before me, I then find it suddenly at my back.' "[14] Yan Hui understood very well what we today call "lifelong learning."

Yan Hui was not successful in practical matters, and his life was cut short. But his devotion to learning made him an enduring exemplar of Confucian education. He lived to learn, and learning was following the Way — not arriving somewhere definitive. The best students understood that the teacher, too, was only on the Way. The best teacher doesn't aspire to arrive at a place; he only wants to learn. And this gives students the permission to improve on the work of the teacher and even to contradict him. "When encountering matters that involve [the basic principles] of humanity," Confucius said, "do not yield even to your teacher." The junzi, we are told, "is agreeable without being an echo. The petty man echoes without being agreeable."[15] The junzi who loves learning can be agreeable without imitating anyone — and that can make the person of stature both a student and a teacher. As we shall see, this combination of fidelity and independence, of being agreeable and also being critical, will be prized in students across the centuries and around the globe.

Socrates was born in 469 BCE, just a few years after Confucius died on the other side of the world. His father was a stone mason and his mother a midwife. The family lived in Alopece, a district of Athens where it was conventional that all males would receive a basic education that would prepare them to participate in civic life. Socrates, like Confucius, benefited from a more extensive education than most, which meant that he received advanced instruction in music, poetry, and athletics. The stone mason also taught his son his trade, though we have little indication that Socrates ever practiced it — unless one considers his conversations in the marketplace his own kind of trade. Various sources tell us that he hung around the Agora (the marketplace) engaging young men in structured discussions about matters great and small. Some of those men (Plato most famously) would become his students, or at least they would one day claim Socrates as their teacher.

Like Confucius, Socrates lived in a time of tumult. Athens, a democratic city-state governed by its free male citizens, was enveloped in a long war with Sparta to its south and engaged in simmering conflicts with Persia to the east. The Peloponnesian War with Sparta lasted from 431 to 404, and Socrates' military duties enhanced his reputation for devotion to his homeland while also compromising him in the eyes of its future leaders. Some of the philosopher's students and friends went over to the side of the Spartan enemy. When Sparta proved victorious, it installed an oligarchic government in Athens known as the Thirty. Although other Greek cities had urged the destruction of Athens, the Spartans thought that rule by the oligarchs could preserve positive aspects of the city-state while ensuring it could no longer threaten its neighbors. The Thirty's tenure was a brutal time of denunciations, land confiscations, and executions. After about eight months of this, the tyrants were overthrown.

Socrates had close associates among the Thirty, but they nonetheless passed rules that prohibited him from pursuing his conversations at the Agora. Still, the lover of wisdom did not flee after the military defeat of Athens, and this was held against him when the tyrants whom the enemy had installed were deposed. But after years of war and violent political infighting, including the execution of thousands, Athenians wanted a peaceful path forward. They swore oaths of amnesty to forget past wrongs, at least the wrongs of politics. Socrates would later be accused of somewhat different offenses, including corrupting youth and impiety toward the gods, but surely the political and military turmoil in his earlier years affected the ways his conversations in the marketplace were perceived.

Philosophers often refer to the "Socrates problem": much of what we know about this figure comes from later philosophers who projected their own ideas back onto him. Socrates did not write down his ideas but rather developed them in conversation with others. While we think of those conversation partners as his students, we should also keep in mind that Socrates famously denied (as did Confucius) that he had anything in particular to teach. Still, it is clear enough for our purposes that he engaged young men (and the occasional woman) in philosophic conversations in which they discovered something about themselves and their relation to the world. It is also clear that he valued nothing more highly than these exchanges. Not even his own life.

What did it mean to be a student of Socrates? Again, we focus on three examples: Xenophon, Plato, and the citizens of Athens. The first, Xenophon, famous for his military exploits, saw Socrates as an example of what it means to lead a virtuous life. The second, Plato, became arguably the greatest teacher in the history of Western philosophy by creating a literary figure out of his mentor and then using this figure as a bottomless philosophical resource. Our third example is not a single student but a group of men described by Socrates as in need of education. These men sentenced their would-be teacher to death and in doing so inadvertently created an educational legacy powerful to this day.

In Xenophon's first encounter with Socrates, the philosopher asked the young man where one might buy some goods, and Xenophon told him. Then Socrates asked him where one might go

---

to improve one's soul, and Xenophon reports that he had no response. Follow me, said the man who would become his teacher, follow me to the marketplace for discussion.

This question of improving one's soul is at the heart of the Socratic enterprise. "I was never acquainted with anyone who took greater care to find out what each of his companions knew," writes Xenophon in the *Memorabilia*.[16] At first glance, Socrates seems here to be the model of the generous interlocutor. Enough about me; how about you? What do you think? But there is a sharp edge to the Socratic interest in what others know. Socrates supposedly turned to philosophy after a trip to the Temple of Delphi, where he was told by the oracle that he was the wisest of men. How can that be? Socrates asked, turning for answers to those around him who were said to be wise. In questioning "his companions," in attempting to find out what they knew, he exposed that they weren't wise at all. Socratic curiosity about what others know is fueled by skepticism, a suspicion that they might not actually know what they think they know. Socrates, at least, was aware of his own ignorance, which we are led to believe is what the oracle had in mind all along.

Xenophon, at least for a time, was one of Socrates' principal interlocutors. A military man, he grew up near Athens in a well-to-do household where he undoubtedly received a decent education, and as a member of the Equestrian class, he was able to ride and hunt and had few obligations. His family estate depended on small shareholders, and it seems that before he became a soldier, he learned to manage these kinds of properties, an experience that doubtless came in handy when his military career was over. And what a military career it was! Part of an ill-fated campaign in Persia, Xenophon was chosen by fellow soldiers to extricate them from a treacherous situation. He managed to make the retreat a success, saving thousands of lives. In carving out the return to Greece, he was not averse to slaughtering those in his way. Nor was he averse to allying himself with those who were once his rivals, even the enemies of his native city, as he would do when going to war on behalf of Sparta. Athens would exile the great general, but his adopted Sparta set him up nicely as a master of a large estate from which he could write about his military exploits, political power, and even horsemanship. He would also paint a powerful picture of his teacher and friend Socrates.

Xenophon was a practical man, and the Socrates he depicts is more interested in ordinary life and reasoning through ordinary problems than is the Socrates portrayed by Plato. In the military leader's accounts, Socrates is less inclined to seek a principle that holds up in all cases than he is to offer worldly advice to someone dealing with a specific issue. Xenophon's teacher in the marketplace also wants his interlocutors to know that they can become better human beings as they become better at dealing with the world. Self-control is a recurrent theme as Socrates urges his conversation partners to learn from hard work, to take pleasure and knowledge from successful toil. *Eupraxia* (well-being) comes from having learned from the successful completion of a difficult task. "The best and the dearest to the gods are, in farming, those who do well in farming affairs and, in medicine, those who do well in medical affairs and, in political life, those who do well in political affairs."[17] Are some tasks intrinsically better than others? Is philosophy better than chariot racing? Xenophon's Socrates chooses philosophy, but he notes that if he were a charioteer, he might have a different view.

Xenophon clearly uses Socrates to voice his own views on mastering the practical affairs of life. The general believed in learning from necessity, in the importance of practice, and in the ability to improve oneself through self-control and attention to the task at hand. And so does his Socrates. He describes his teacher playfully pushing these beliefs to an extreme in his conversation with the courtesan Theodote. In prior sections of this book of Xenophon's *Memorabilia*, Socrates has talked with a painter, a craftsman, and a maker of armor. Now it's the beautiful Theodote, who offers men pleasure in return for financial support. And she is very well supported. When Socrates hears from one of his students that Theodote's beauty surpasses many things, including speech, he responds playfully, "We must go to behold her, for surely it is not possible for those who have merely heard to learn what surpasses speech."[18]

Once in Theodote's presence, Socrates begins discussing her with the young men he has brought with him: does she benefit more from being adored, or do the men benefit more from the pleasure of adoring her? Living quite modestly himself, Socrates takes note of her wealth — her fine clothes, her well-appointed entourage. "How does she come by her wealth?" he inquires. And she responds, "If someone who has become my friend wants to treat me well, he is my livelihood." Well, then, says the master teacher, how does she go about getting men to become her friends — how does she get them to follow her and support her? Spiders weave webs to get what they need for sustenance, and hunters make elaborate preparations to catch their prey. "And what sort of nets," she responds, "have I?" "To be sure, one that is indeed very entangling: your body," he answers. "And in it a soul, through which you learn both how you might gratify with a look and delight with what you say; and that you must receive with gladness one who is attentive but shut out one who is spoiled." Here Socrates is pointing out how powerful a seeker of friends Theodote must be — and then she turns the point back upon him in noticing that he, too, has followers. Perhaps he can procure the right kinds of friends for her! The philosopher is sometimes described as a matchmaker, and she jokingly invites him to be her pimp.[19]

Socrates replies to Theodote that he does indeed have love charms, and then, underscoring the main point of their exchange, adds that it makes no sense to try to attract those who have no need of what one is offering. It makes no sense, in other words, to try to attract those who have no desire. People who are fully satiated will turn away from even delectable food. Whether one is in the business of philosophy or of bodily pleasure, one must wait until the right moment when the potential friend feels desire: "You neither approach nor offer any reminder to those who are satiated until they stop being full and are in need again. Then, . . . you offer reminders to those who are in need by means of the most decorous intimacy possible and by visibly wishing to gratify . . . [but then] flee until they are desirous. For it makes a big difference to give the same gifts at that point, rather than before they desire them."[20]

Is not Xenophon here offering a commentary on the gifts of education as well? Only when people know they are in need of learning, only when they begin to recognize their own ignorance, will they have the desire necessary for education. And that is when they become students. "It makes a big difference," Socrates and Theodote agree, "to approach a human being according to nature and correctly."[21] Feeling one's hunger for learning, recognizing one's incapacities, will lead one to the gifts of the caring teacher.

Recognition of one's own ignorance is at the heart of Plato's figure of Socrates. This is the iconic portrait of the founder of philosophy whose persistent questioning makes one realize that one's own beliefs have no firm foundation. Now, it's certainly the case that

Plato's Socrates advances doctrines, and that Platonic philosophy makes claims about topics ranging from cosmology to ethics. But it's also true that every Western philosophical school traces its lineage to Socrates and his students — whether they are the most stoical or the most hedonistic. Questioning, what would become known as the Socratic method, is common to these traditions, and it is on this questioning that we will focus in our discussion of how the student Plato imagined his teacher.

In Plato's dialogues, Socrates asks his interlocutors whether they are really as sure of themselves as they seem to be. Sometimes he probes whether they truly understand the words they are using, whether their claim to authority or expertise is based on knowledge or just habit or illusion. The students of Socrates aren't the only ones questioned. At times it seems Socrates will query anyone he can find! But the intentional students learn from this as well by watching as others engaged by their teacher are schooled, whether they like it or not, and realize that their certainties are misplaced.

At his fateful trial, Socrates claimed that his questioning was mocked by his "first accusers": Athenians, embarrassed at having had their ignorance exposed, fabricated a false and poisonous picture "telling of one Socrates, a wise man, who speculated about the heaven above, and searched into the earth beneath, and made the worse appear the better cause." Socrates objected, arguing that the simple truth was that he never discussed such subjects "to any extent at all."[22] Nor, he emphasized in his own defense, did he impart his teaching in exchange for pay.

No, but Socrates is proud to possess knowledge of his own ignorance and the ability to expose the ignorance of others. He is better off than those he questions; Socrates claims, "The error of theirs [overconfidence in their knowledge] overshadowed their wisdom."

Socrates describes his own "slight advantage" to the citizens who will decide his fate at the climactic trial portrayed in Plato's *Apology:* the ignorance displayed to his students. They learn something altogether vital (and perhaps a little dangerous): money doesn't make you wise, and power doesn't make you virtuous. With money and power you may rise in the esteem of others, but Socratic questioning may well reveal that this esteem is built on a foundation of sand. In Plato's dialogues, Socrates relates that in making visible the ignorance of others he is fulfilling his obligation to the oracle. He is showing that many who claim to speak from a position of knowledge, who may appear to be wise, don't really know what they are talking about. This is his occupation, as he says, and young people around him "like to hear the cross-examination of the pretenders to wisdom; there is amusement in it."[23] Obviously, not everyone was amused.

It's easy enough to understand the animosity of those esteemed citizens of Athens who found their own ignorance exposed in front of a group of young men pleased to see their so-called betters taken down a peg or two. And it was doubtless irritating to see Socrates display his "wisdom" without having to support any position, only having to show that his conversation partner's position was erroneous. As the Sophist Thrasymachus put it: "Socrates can carry on as usual. He gives no answer himself but pulls to pieces the answer of someone else." The Sophists were itinerant teachers who traveled in the Greek city-states in the second half of the fifth century BCE instructing young people in the arts of rhetoric and inquiry in return for fees. Later philosophers would often portray the Sophists as promoting mere persuasion as opposed to the clear pursuit of truth or wisdom. Plato's Socrates is critical of the Sophists for emphasizing the powers of speech and argument, skills that can easily mask ignorance about principles and goals. In the first book of Plato's *Republic,* the tough-minded Thrasymachus is provoked by young men who continue to hang on Socrates' every word even as he undermines their ideas of justice without offering any idea of his own. Thrasymachus retorts: "That's just Socrates' usual irony. I knew . . . that you [Socrates] would be unwilling to answer and that if someone questioned *you*, you'd be ironical and do anything rather than give an answer." When Socrates goes on to question the Sophist's own description of justice as the right of the stronger, the latter complains that his questioner is acting abominably by "taking the words in the sense that is most damaging to the argument."[24] Socrates defends himself, and eventually Thrasymachus calms down.

Much was at stake in facing the skeptical questions of Socrates, and not just social esteem. In ancient Athens, the concept of *Eusebia,* a combination of piety and conforming to social mores, was integral to how citizens understood civic duty. In doing one's duty, performing the civic rituals that held daily life together, many things "go without saying." Loyalty involved maintaining one's connections to one's group — family, tribe, city — and loyalty was a crucial dimension of Eusebia. This dimension was sorely tested by the military and political conflicts that erupted during Socrates' lifetime. During the wars with Sparta, Xenophon was not the only one associated with the philosopher who was sympathetic with (or overtly fought for) Athens' rival city. So did Alcibiades, whose life is said to have been saved by Socrates in their youth. Alcibiades defected to the Spartan side during the Peloponnesian War, and then to Persia before returning to the Athenian side. The Athenians who would eventually stand in judgment of Socrates for "corrupting the youth of the city" remembered that some of his students had proved all too ready to abandon Eusebia. Had Socrates taught them to ironically "pull to pieces" the received wisdom of the polity without ever providing them with another reason to be loyal? Did being a student of Socrates mean that you were above loyalty to *anything?*

Plato's dialogue *Euthyphro* deals explicitly with loyalty and piety. On his way to answer a charge of impiety made against him, Socrates runs into Euthyphro, who is himself headed to court to accuse his own father of causing the death of a servant. Pretending to be impressed by the younger man's certainty that it is perfectly pious to lodge a charge against one's own father, Socrates asks rather ironically for instruction in the ways of reverence so that he may successfully answer the charges of impiety against himself. The ensuing dialogue shows how the young man really has little sense of how to define piety (Euthyphro's claim is that piety is whatever pleases the gods) and thus should not be trusted with the practice of it. The word *euthyphro* means "straight thinker" in Greek, and in this dialogue the irony is especially intense as the overconfident young man goes round in circles, forced to return again and again to his obviously inadequate definition of piety.

Plato's *Euthyphro* dialogue is fun to read in part because its main character is so obtuse — he keeps exemplifying the impiety of overconfidence. Overconfidence is not a minor problem in Socrates' eyes — it is a vital human failing because it gets in the way of learning. Learning through recognizing one's own ignorance is an essential dimension of being a student; indeed, it is an essential human capacity, and poor Euthyphro's almost comic intellectual arrogance makes him the opposite of a student. He seems immune to learning. To be open to learning, one must give up one's assurances, or at least some of them.[25]

The Socratic irony at work here is more subtle than may first appear. Sure, we, the readers, can tell that Euthyphro is conceited, too sure of himself, unchanged by the encounter with the master teacher.

———

How about us? Do we read this dialogue only to feel better about ourselves for recognizing Euthyphro's boneheadedness? Reading the dialogue may give us a false sense of confidence: at least we are not as bad as Euthyphro. Students working through the dialogue find it easy to side with Socrates, but that may lead one to a false sense of intellectual confidence—the very thing that siding with Socrates is supposed to prevent! We never do get a satisfying definition of piety in this dialogue, so how are *we* to break out of the circle that Euthyphro found himself in? In enjoying the bad student's comeuppance, we may not realize that we are not so different from him.[26] How do we turn the Socratic questioning back on ourselves to become better students than Euthyphro? What would it mean for us to do so?

Centuries of commentaries on these questions emphasize that self-questioning and the intellectual humility it should bring are essential aspects of learning as an open-ended process of inquiry. In book VII of Plato's *Republic,* Socrates underscores the challenges of that process, likening us to prisoners in a cave, enchained and able to look only in a single direction, where we see shadows projected on a wall. Since that is all we see, all we know, we take the shadows for real things rather than mere shadows. An education through philosophy helps us understand when we are looking in the wrong direction—when the conventional ways we direct our attention will not show us the essential things. This education, Socrates emphasizes, must overcome the habituation of our senses: it's easy for our senses to mistake the shadows for reality and to resist seeing things in their true light. We might even fear or punish those who do see truly, treating them as threats to our way of life as we remain among the shadows in our caves.

Students who learn, says Plato's Socrates, will strive to ascend from the world of shadows, the realm of appearances. This is different from desiring mere instruction, as if one could "put knowledge into the soul which was not there before." No, a true education recognizes that the power to learn is present in everyone's soul and the instrument with which each learns is like an eye that cannot be turned from darkness to light without turning the whole body.[27] Education of the "whole soul" is a turning away from mere appearances and toward the good. This turning, for Plato's Socrates, is accomplished only as one comes to recognize that one has been paying attention to the wrong things, only as one comes to recognize one's own ignorance.[28] Xenophon, by contrast, sees his teacher Socrates as someone who can point out the pretensions of others while also helping his interlocutors gain insights they can apply in their ordinary lives. You don't have to turn away from your mundane occupation to learn from Xenophon's teacher; you have only to pay attention differently. Plato's Socrates is a teacher with a dangerous message, and his most famous student would want to protect that message by removing it from the center of the action. It's Plato, after all, who takes philosophical practice from the public marketplace to an academy where students can more safely turn their intellectual attentions to philosophical problems. Plato is a student who sees his teacher as a master who unmasks the ignorance of others and a philosopher who shows the pathway out of the cave-like darkness of their ordinary lives for something more true, more good. Not all of the interlocutors Plato depicts in his dialogues learn from Socrates; it is the readers of the dialogues who are the real students. And readers can study more safely at the academy.

Socrates' students were not just those who conversed with him, wrote about him, or read those writings. The iconic philosopher took the citizens of Athens as his students — or at least he was forced to when they put him on trial. Between wars with Sparta and

Persia and the overthrow of democracy at home, this was a trying time for a city once so proud of its ability to govern itself with strength and prudence. And Socrates was a natural target. Plato's *Apology* gives one account of Socrates' defense in front of a "jury" of five hundred fellow citizens. Xenophon, too, describes the defense, featuring a belligerent Socrates who dares the Athenian jurors to sentence him to death even as he underscores his superiority to them. Plato's Socrates doesn't force the jury's hand, but neither does he apologize for the practice of philosophy. Rather than make the expected plea for mercy, Socrates argues that the city would be the better off allowing this philosophical practice to continue. Or perhaps it is Plato who is trying to convince his readers that any collectivity would be fortunate to have a provocative public philosopher in its midst, encouraging its members to become clearer about what they know — and what they don't.

Socrates had performed honorable military service, but his fame came from his very public questioning of prominent Athenians, and he was doubtless well known to the jury for that reason. Plato's Socrates made no bones about his skepticism regarding reputation. "I found that those who had the highest reputation were really the most deficient, while those who were thought to be inferior were more knowledgeable." This in itself might reasonably have been taken as undermining Eusebia, the conventions of the city. But Socrates — careful that his contempt for the city's notables not be taken as simple impiety — claimed that his mission of exposing ignorance in fact stemmed from his obedience to the gods. It was the oracle who pushed him to show "that the wisdom of men is worth little or nothing": "I go around seeking anyone, citizen or stranger, whom I think wise. Then if I do not think he is, I come to the assistance of the god and show him that he is not wise." Socrates aims to convince his fellow citizens that the practice of philosophy is a higher piety. The poets, rhetoricians, politicians, and craftsmen are all angry at him for having exposed what they failed to understand. Socrates doesn't claim to have some deep understanding – only to reveal its absence in others, and for that he is unapologetic: He emphasizes that the hatred of those whose ignorance he has exposed is just further proof of the importance of his obedience to the god.[29] Does Socrates here really expect the jury to accept this as a defense of the philosophical way of life, or is this just Plato's way of appealing to a jury of future readers – a jury of future students who would learn the art of questioning?

The Athenian citizens who sat in judgment on Socrates might have expected an appeal for mercy, for such was the convention in these sorts of hearings. Instead, they heard a defiant philosopher declare that he would continue to practice his questioning out of obedience to a god, for he was unafraid of being put to death. Since we don't know what death brings, he tells his fellow citizens, it is foolish to fear it.[30] He teases the jurors, saying that instead of killing him, they might consider putting him in the place of heroes, the Prytaneum (with free meals), but he also lashes out, predicting that the city will one day suffer because it has prevented the exposure of the intellectual and moral dishonesty of those with money, prestige, and power.

Plato's Socrates pleads not for his own life but for the good that the philosopher does for the state. He jokes that he is a gift to his fellow citizens: "I was attached to the city by a god . . . as upon a great and noble horse which was somewhat sluggish because of its size and needed to be stirred by a kind of gadfly." He insists that if they don't spare him, they won't easily replace him. Of course they do not, but Socrates remains defiant: "You are wrong if you believe that by killing people you will prevent anyone from reproaching you for not living the right way."[31] But perhaps *defiant* isn't quite the right word since the philosopher accepts the verdict of the jury and refuses to make any effort to evade his execution. He doesn't reject the Eusebia of his city so much as work to improve it by having his fellow citizens reflect on what they do. He gathers his students around him until the end, explaining why it is important that he not flee the executioner. In his last hours, surrounded by his students, the condemned philosopher affirms the value of argument, of conversation, and of remaining a citizen of one's city by accepting its rulings.

Plato's dialogue was meant to make students of his readers, arming them with queries and arguments that expose ignorance but also affirming loyalty to a philosophical way of life and to a city that might yet learn from it.

Jesus of Nazareth also lived in turbulent times. Palestine in the first century before the Common Era was occupied by Rome, which placed a heavy yoke on the Jewish population. The Jews had a long history of foreign invasion and occupation, having had to rebuild the destroyed Temple in Jerusalem (around 200 BCE) and deal with the threat of Hellenization for centuries. Different forms of Judaism existed in response to foreign influences, including strict observance of the Law as it was written in the sacred texts of the Torah. During Jesus's time, some would make this observance a private matter, striving for minimal conflict with the corrupt and brutal Roman authorities. Others used their Judaism zealously to spark resistance against those occupying the Holy Land.

Jesus began his teaching in this atmosphere of political and military strife, which was all but inseparable from religious and cultural turmoil. And it was as a teacher that he was encountered – an itinerant rabbi or preacher who mesmerized followers with parables, interpretations of the Law and, according to his apostles, extraordinary deeds. He is said to turn corrupt men away from their illicit business dealings, heal the sick, feed the hungry, and even walk on water. As Jesus begins to teach during the harvest festival of Succoth, the people, according to the book of John, "marveled, saying: 'How is it that this man has learning, when he has never studied?' " The teacher's answer is revealing: "My teaching is not mine, but his who sent me. If anyone's will is to do God's will, he will know whether the teaching is from God or whether I am speaking on my own authority. The one who speaks on his own authority seeks his own glory; but the one who seeks the glory of him who sent him is true, and in him there is no falsehood" (John 7:17).

Jesus claims to be no ordinary teacher; he is not offering an interpretation of the Law or even of God's word. What this teacher asks of students is to be followers, for his teaching is offered as the embodiment of the Lord who sent him. The word made flesh, as one will later say, rather than only an intellectual message. Mere understanding of the teaching is not enough; these students are asked to change their ways and walk in the path that their teacher has set out. We'll briefly consider his most famous students: Peter, who becomes the rock on which the teaching is built for posterity; Matthew, the tax collector who represents the transformative power of the teaching; Judas, who betrays his teacher; and Paul, who is converted to a missionary zealously sharing the teaching as the Good News.

Peter (also called Simon) is often described as the first or lead apostle of Jesus. In the Gospel according to Mark, Jesus walks by Peter and Andrew, a pair of brother fishermen in Galilee, and bids them to follow him – and to fish for people in the future. Another account has Jesus enter Peter's house to heal the disciple's mother-in-law, while the book of John has the two meeting shortly after Jesus is singled out as the Messiah by John the Baptist. The personality of Peter that emerges from these accounts is of a simple fisherman who is called to witness extraordinary events, a student who is sometimes baffled or intimidated by these occurrences, only to be brought back to his teacher's path through profound faith. Is this teacher really the Messiah, many asked? Jesus puts the question directly to those who wanted to be his students or disciples: " 'Who do you say I am?' Peter (Simon) responds: 'Thou art Christ, the Son of the living God.' And Jesus answering said to him: 'Blessed art thou, Simon Bar-Jona: because flesh and blood hath not revealed it to thee, but my Father who is in heaven. And I say to thee: That thou art Peter [Kipha, a rock], and upon this rock I will build my church, and the gates of hell shall not prevail against it. And I will give to thee the keys of the kingdom of heaven' " (Matthew 16:17–19).

The commission Jesus gives Peter becomes the foundation for centuries of popes, but even a rock will sometimes falter. When Jesus tells Peter at the Last Supper that his favored disciple will betray him, Peter is indignant, but of course in the coming hours he will sleep when his teacher is in anguish and then, fearful for his own safety, deny he knows him. The story of Peter shows that one does not have to be perfect or pure to be a follower of the Son of God. Purity is not an option in this world, and faith comes through acknowledging weakness. Peter is a rock, but even a rock has fissures. Being a student of Jesus means accepting that one will never be a perfect student.

Perhaps it was to underscore this point that Jesus chose the tax collector Matthew as one of his cherished disciples. In Roman-dominated Palestine, local contractors could acquire the privilege of collecting money or crops on behalf of the government; unsurprisingly, they were generally despised and often classified with harlots and criminals. Jesus, asked by the Pharisees and the teachers of the law, "Why do you eat and drink with tax collectors and sinners?" answered: "It is not the healthy who need a doctor, but the sick. I have not come to call the righteous, but sinners to repentance." And so the tale is as simple as this: he saw Matthew sitting at the tax collector's booth, told him, "Follow me," and Matthew got up and followed him" (Luke 5:31–32).

Jesus would be a teacher not of "gifted" students but of sinners in need of following a new way. Confucius pointed out the strengths and weaknesses of those who followed him, striving to develop his students' capacities and reduce their flaws. Socrates was willing to expose the intellectual pretensions of anyone, and he took particular delight in unmasking those who really believed they were gifted. But Jesus took this much further, seeking out those whom others despised, or at least those who had suffered in life. Since his teaching offered such profound redemption, his students' neediness, their deficits, were really an advantage. In Matthew's case, his despised profession did grant him one advantage: he knew how to write. According to tradition, Matthew was the first to transcribe Jesus's teachings.

Below, Matthew lists the first four of the Eight Beatitudes—blessings that Jesus teaches in the Sermon on the Mount—which might be said to describe how weaknesses become virtues or blessings:

Blessed are the poor in spirit,
for theirs is the kingdom of heaven.

Blessed are those who mourn,
for they will be comforted.

Blessed are the meek,
for they will inherit the earth.

Blessed are those who hunger and thirst for righteousness,
for they will be filled. (Matthew 5:3–10)

The turning of the corrupt or weak toward righteousness and salvation is fundamental to Jesus's teaching and a departure from Jewish tradition and Greek philosophy. But not all those who are corrupt are saved, and one student famously turned the other way, against the teacher and his teachings. This teacher knew he would be betrayed and said as much (three times) at the Last Supper. Although Jesus didn't name Judas Iscariot directly as his betrayer, Judas confirmed his master's foreboding with a kiss — signaling to the authorities that Jesus was the rebellious preacher they were looking for. He also referred publicly to Jesus as his teacher, his rabbi.

Unlike the other apostles, we are not told how Jesus asked Judas to follow him. Readers of the Scriptures are warned only that Judas is a "devil" who will eventually betray his teacher. In the book of John, Judas is rebuked by his teacher for not understanding why he allowed a sinful woman to anoint his feet. When Judas complains that the luxurious ointment could have been sold and the money used to care for the poor, Jesus says to leave her alone: "It was intended that she should save this perfume for the day of my burial" (John 12:7). Many commentaries tie this woman's profound love for Jesus to the deep forgiveness he would accord her. Judas is the student who cannot grasp this kind of redemption; he thinks only of the missed transaction that might have helped the cause. The kind of learning that leads to love and redemption is beyond Judas, who will later infamously accept thirty pieces of silver for betraying his teacher. In the book of Luke, it is said that "Satan entered" the failed student, the one who fell away from following (Luke 22:3).

The apostle Paul never met Jesus — at least not when his teacher was alive. But arguably Paul became the most influential of his students — a grand missionary for his master's teachings. Paul, also known by his Hebrew name Saul, probably came from a devout Jewish family. He studied in centers of learning with the great teachers of the age, and as a young man he proved his religious devotion by persecuting Christians as heretics. But it was on the road to Damascus, well after the crucifixion, that he had the revelation of a higher Truth that would change his life — and alter the course of history.

Saul was nearing the end of his journey to Damascus when a blinding light suddenly came from the sky. Falling from his horse, he heard a voice asking, "Saul, Saul, why do you persecute me?" Confused and frightened, Saul asked who was speaking and was told it was Jesus. His traveling companions heard things, too, but they did not understand what was happening. As Saul struggled to his feet, he was instructed, "Go to the city, and you will be told what you must do" (Acts 9:4–6). Saul found that he could see nothing, and his companions had to lead him the rest of the way to Damascus. He remained blind for three days until healed by Ananias, ordered by Jesus in a vision to restore Saul's sight. The restoration of sight symbolizes the embodied understanding of the teaching. In a flash, the conversion is complete; the persecutor has become the student/ follower. And then a new, different kind of teacher: the proselytizer.

The teachings of Jesus were not calls to return to tradition, like the lessons of Confucius; nor were they conversational encounters that revealed what one didn't know, like the questions of Socrates. The teachings of Jesus were meant to turn one toward another life, a life in which you would leave behind the person you had been and be born again as a follower of God's Messiah. Perhaps "teachings" is the wrong word for the kind of revelation that knocks one to the ground, that blinds one to one's previous life and launches one in a completely new direction. To be a student of Jesus meant to be open to the message of love that the teacher embodied, and to be receptive to the power with which it was delivered. Jesus takes the transformative dimension of learning to a different level. The student as disciple is someone who is so receptive as to be ready for rebirth.

With our three students of Confucius, the teachings of the master intersected with *who they were* without offering them a fully new life. Each of the three represents a different personality type, and each learned differently. The teacher, to use a contemporary phrase, "met them where they were." Similarly, each of Socrates' students also had a particular relationship to the master's mode of questioning; what they had in common was taking to heart critique and the intellectual modesty that should go along with it. Although they might have been transformed by the irony that their teacher brought to established hierarchies in the city, they were not given a new doctrine with which to reorient their lives. The student in the Christian tradition, in contrast, becomes the ardent follower, filled with love and with the conviction that one's new direction is *the* direction that all should follow. The student in this new tradition is not just a faithful follower but also a missionary, one who bears the Good News, the teachings of the Son of God, for all who have ears to hear.

Chapter 2

CHILDREN, APPRENTICES, STUDENTS

Learning Independence

Across the centuries, students have encountered modes of learning of the kinds associated with Confucius, Socrates, and Jesus: those that promised harmonious integration, critical self-awareness, or renewal through the acceptance of a mentor's path. These encounters often lead to questions. Am I supposed to learn skills from my teacher, or is it a way of life that I am to follow? Am I to remain faithful to my teacher, or am I supposed to "graduate" from being a student to being self-reliant, even rebellious? Following more ordinary teachers, more ordinary students were typically learning how to achieve some independence but also how to play a part in their communities with purpose. Even before the development of widespread schooling, young people were expected to learn how to become economically independent while also fitting in with traditions and hierarchies. Being a student meant developing the agency to participate in one's ecosystem, be that a family, village, town, or city. If in the premodern West being a student usually meant developing the independence necessary for fitting into one's society, at the dawn of the modern period students were increasingly pictured as people who were learning to think for themselves. Thinking for oneself would become part of what it meant to *be* a person. People prevented from learning were those whose very humanity was denied by their societies. They could not be students because they were slaves. The denial of educational possibilities to the category of the slave paradoxically pointed to the link that would emerge in the modern period between being a student and learning to be free.

The label "medieval Europe" encompasses a wide range of space and time. The eastern part of the continent in the fifth century, for instance, didn't have the same customs and conventions as the Iberian Peninsula four hundred years later. The premodern West was multifarious, and it changed unevenly over a millennium. In this chapter we will look only at characteristic examples of young people educated, usually by parents, before the widespread development of schools and literacy. As educational institutions in Europe were just developing, what did it mean for a young person in medieval Europe to grow up? What did learning have to do with this process?

In much of Europe during the Middle Ages, young people could pursue apprenticeships in addition to and occasionally instead of learning within their families. In apprenticeships they'd learn specific skills from an older person who had already mastered them and been certified to take on trainees. Acquiring these skills would prepare the apprentice to practice a craft or a trade. With successful practice came the ability to be independent from one's teacher or master. Ideally, it also paved the way to becoming a master or teacher oneself. Apprenticeships were very specific, but already in the medieval period there were students enrolled in schools that taught not only a trade but the art of learning itself. Students were recognized

by religious and sometimes civil authorities as people whose vocation was learning, apart from the ability to acquire specific skills.
They were meant to develop capacities to acquire knowledge even
prior to the wide dissemination of books and the development of
formal disciplines.

When I was a pursuing a PhD in history in the late 1970s and early
'80s, social history was seen as a powerful vehicle for understanding
the past on its own terms. Social historians wanted to cure the profession of presentism, by which they meant that researchers should
stop projecting their assumptions onto the lives of people who lived
long ago. Things taken for granted or deemed "natural" today might
actually be creations of specific times and places, and we shouldn't
assume that because we value something now, people in the past
valued that same thing. Freedom, for example, meant something
quite different in the eleventh-century Holy Roman Empire than it
did in twentieth-century Vienna. Same goes for faith or success or
love – or being a student.

    It was in this spirit of anti-presentism that in 1960 French so-
cial historian Philippe Ariès announced that there was no such thing
as childhood in medieval Europe. By this he meant that prior to the
modern age, youngsters were not seen as specific *kinds* of people
with distinct needs and characteristics. Childhood, said Ariès, was an
invention of the modern era, and we should refrain from projecting
that invention back onto earlier historical periods. After all, before
the eighteenth century, when so many babies did not live to see their
first birthday, it just wasn't wise to invest emotionally or economically in these small, vulnerable humans. The category of "childhood"
was created only after it became safe enough to care about the very

young. Social historians were triumphant in pointing out that something so many regarded as "natural," affection for babies, was actually a product of historical conditions such as improved hygiene.[1]

In the last couple of decades, however, scholars have pushed back against this view that childhood did not exist before infant mortality rates decreased. Recent historians have argued that ideas and practices in the distant past might sometimes have resembled our own. In fact, medieval parents often doted on their kids, and even when faced with challenging economic conditions, they tried to find ways to provide for their youngest family members. With respect to medieval England, historian Barbara Hanawalt judges that the oral traditions that have come down to us and the practices we can learn about from archival sources that portray village practices indicate "coherent moral values for the protection of vulnerable children." Part of this set of values was teaching the young what they would need to know to survive in the world. In the absence of state-sponsored education, parents "understood that their children's survival depended on their resources and training," writes Hanawalt.[2] The first task was to keep them alive, which in the precarious world of the Middle Ages meant getting enough food and avoiding such dangers as walking on thin ice or playing with fire. And there were dangers aplenty. Mortality rates were highest in the first years of life; in medieval England about 40 percent of children perished before they were ten years old.[3]

Young children were vulnerable, and they were not typically viewed as fully responsible for the risks they ran. Throughout Christian Europe, they were baptized as soon as possible and then deemed incapable of intentional sin until they reached puberty, at around age twelve for girls and age fourteen for boys. Religion, law, and local mores encouraged young people to learn what it meant to

———

be a responsible adult while still allowing some flexibility for the inevitable mistakes.[4] Stories were recited to instill in children the basic moral virtues of the time — much as children's books do today. Narratives were meant to educate, and they circulated in religious and secular settings. Fables that underscored the benefits of honesty and hard work (and the poor outcomes of lying and laziness) were known to young and old.[5] Of course, only a small minority of the population was able to read. Around 1400, a market began to develop for the publication of stories aimed at people of various ages, but it would be centuries before literacy became widespread.

With little or no formal schooling, most students were simply learning to enter adulthood, to gain the skills to establish and support their own families. Most households in northern Europe, for instance, consisted of two generations (parents and children), while in southern Europe one finds more multigenerational homes. Historians have found plenty of evidence that families in much of medieval Europe devoted affection and attention to very young children; often their first years were a time in which family members consciously used play as a vehicle for teaching safe habits. Parents tried to protect their offspring by carving out a world safe enough for exploration — and their grief was intense when they failed to do so.[6] Parents were aware of the precariousness of young lives, but this did not make them care for their children less. The first seven years or so of life were viewed as a stage of mutual discovery: parents found out about the nature of their children, and children discovered how to express that nature. The next phase of life, beginning at about seven years old and proceeding through puberty into young adulthood, was considered the best for learning. St. Anselm argued that the very young were like wax that was too soft and couldn't really be molded, whereas the very old had already hardened into their permanent shapes and couldn't easily learn new things; but older children and adolescents were "like wax which is neither soft nor hard, and hence can be instructed and educated."[7]

In peasant families, children were laborers. Families hoped for offspring—but not too many. "Excess" children would be hired out to other households who could afford them (and make use of their labor). By age eight or so, boys and girls could perform simple functions within the home or in the fields, like gathering firewood, protecting crops, or minding smaller children. At that time the marriage age was relatively late (for women in their mid-twenties, for men their late twenties). Unmarried youth had to learn how to contribute to the peasant ecosystem, taking on more adult tasks as they became physically stronger. Learning was imitation, and "graduation" was becoming independent through inheriting land or acquiring the ability to marry so as to set up another household that could sustain itself.[8] Survival required nothing less.

Learning to eventually survive without teachers/parents was the primary goal of education in the premodern West. Parents were encouraged by religion and custom to be nurturing, to be sure, but the goal was practical as much as sentimental: to help children build the capacity to contribute to the household and ultimately be able to leave it. There is ample evidence of parental affection but, as Hanawalt emphasizes, "the society was well aware that sentiment could be misleading, and that self-sufficiency was ultimately more important. If children were to learn survival, they might themselves have more of a sense of survival than of love."[9] Children could expect to lose one or both of their parents before they reached adulthood, so developing independence was essential.

But independence was not synonymous with individualism, as it is in many Western societies today. A person's independence was always understood in the context of some community. In addition to learning prudence and household skills, for example, the young were expected to learn respect for custom and hierarchy. Like the followers of Confucius at another time and place, young people were expected to harmoniously integrate into a tradition that prized order. Obedience to one's parents was a commandment sanctified by religion and enforced in daily life. Age itself gave authority, as did wealth and religion. Children learned the hierarchy and their own place within it. There were village big shots, regional noblemen and local clergy, and the commoner families had to teach their young that disturbing the lines of authority could have significant repercussions.

Many young people entered into service or apprenticeship at some distance from their homes. Whether or not children were sent off was usually determined by whether they could meaningfully contribute to the family economy or were a drain on it. In England, where sending children out to service was quite common, poor families would commit a child to, say, work for a farmer from age nine until twenty-one. In exchange for room and board, the youngster was supposed to help with farm tasks. No particular education was part of the deal, though of course one did learn skills that might be useful in another household—or, if one was lucky, one's own. The apprenticeship system was contractual: a family with a "surplus" teenager would sign a contract with another family that required the support of the adolescent, binding the teen to the new household, in exchange for obedience, labor, and good behavior. Girls would typically be domestics, performing household chores and sometimes minding younger children or herding animals.[10] For girls, apart from a contract, the difference between the duties of a servant and those of an apprentice was not always clear. Apprenticed boys would also be servants, although their chores might take them farther from hearth and home. In contributing to their new households, apprentices — boys and girls — were expected to improve in their work over time. A formal apprenticeship promised to impart a more specific set of skills — the young novice learned a trade (or a craft) from a master. Examples included carpentry, brewing, weaving, candle making, learning how to fix tools or to build a chimney.

Many apprenticeships involved negotiations and detailed contracts. We often learn about them from official records of later disputes between the parties that required formal intervention. The young person is learning a trade from someone who is expert at it — at least that's the supposition. The agreements spelled out how much work was required and how much responsibility the master's family took for the well-being of the young person now part of the household. What happened if the adolescent fell ill or was injured? How to ensure there would be enough to eat, or that accommodations would be suitable? These details were often stipulated in the contract.

Additionally, apprenticeship contracts in premodern Europe spelled out moral requirements. The apprentice took an oath not to marry (and also not to fornicate), and there were to be no romantic relations with anyone in the master's house.[11] Contracts went on to describe the importance of resisting temptation, avoiding corrupt company, and not engaging in any activities that would bring discredit to the master, his trade, or his family. In addition to learning a specific trade, the apprentice should also learn how to be a community member in good standing.

Historians have found plenty of reports of unruly and even outright rebellious apprentices. Those in authority worried about how to instill respect for hierarchy and responsible behavior in young people more interested in socializing and drinking. Elder tradesmen did not want their guilds polluted by tempestuous youths, and pious clergy worried about young people away from their parents losing all sense of morality. What was one to do with apprentices who forgot their proper place? Did they need to be beaten more often? Or perhaps, on the contrary, were they subject to too many rules? "Medieval moralists, city fathers, and masters were perplexed," Hanawalt concludes, "about what to do with adolescents."[12] Some things don't change all that much!

Acquiring independence was the goal of the student as an apprentice, just as it was the goal of children growing up in their own households. In the case of the apprentice, there was an added emphasis on the social community. Becoming independent as a member of a trade guild, a village, a town, a church meant learning to leave the world of children, which had its own rather different standards of behavior.[13] Apprentices had to at least appear to grow up and accept their place in a hierarchy imposed by custom and authority. The phrase "premodern Europe" refers to many different regions over many hundreds of years, and naturally the experiences of apprentices could be different in different times and places. In late medieval London, larger firms would accept only boys in their mid-teens, while a century later in Barcelona children at age ten — boys and girls — would commonly be assigned to learn a trade or help out with domestic duties. We know that in Renaissance Florence middle-class families took in children even younger than ten to help with the household's work in exchange for a commitment to help them marry later on.[14] While apprenticeships had core elements in common, the lived experiences of apprentices as students learning the rules of the world varied tremendously.

Wherever or whenever young people began their apprentice-ships, the goal was to acquire the knowledge that masters had of their craft. This was not usually the kind of knowledge that could be found in books. Apprentices were students who learned through practice, and masters had to find ways to continue to remain productive in their craft while imparting skills that their students would need to take up the craft themselves. "Such training led to what might be called an 'artisanal literacy,' " writes historian of science, technology, and artisanal practices Pamela H. Smith. She has emphasized that these students learned in ways that "had to do with gaining knowledge neither through reading nor writing but rather through a process of experience and labor."[15] It was through repetitive labor that the apprentice began to acquire knowledge as habit—knowledge ingrained so deeply in the body that the young artisan could perform at a high level even without the presence of the master. This would be true for sewing or painting, brewing or carpentry.

Let's say a teenage boy in seventeenth-century England travels from the countryside to London to apprentice with a master tailor. How did his parents make the connection to the big city in the first place? Perhaps he had cousins in London, an older brother who had already made his way there, or acquaintances he had met through commerce. By the 1600s in England (and in other parts of western Europe in the latter part of the century), networks of trade were growing, and apprenticeships were part of those networks.[16] When our apprentice finished learning his trade, he would be in his mid-twenties and ideally have acquired both knowledge and connections to put his experience to work.

Apprentices who completed their term had the legal right to pursue their trade, though competition and market pressure often forced them to move to different locales. Ideally, they would be able to use the networks of the master, even if this meant staying less independent as they earned a living through their practice. But the incentive of moving on to a trade that allowed for economic independence was often not great enough to make up for the prolonged subservience to a master. Many apprentices failed to finish their term. According to some historians, between one-third and one-half of apprentices in the seventeenth century "dropped out."[17] The master had authority over the apprentice; as would later also be said of teachers in schools, he was *in loco parentis*. The pressures to obey the master, the difficulties of working and living under someone else's authority, and the distance from family made the apprenticeship process a challenge for many.

Most apprenticeships went to young boys with agreements signed by their fathers. Many guilds, especially in northern Europe, forbade young women from entering a trade as apprentices, and for years historians regarded this system as yet one more means of patriarchal control. However, recent studies exploring the world of female apprentices have looked at ways in which girls entered trades to learn the skills necessary for *their* own independence. Sometimes they would employ these skills after starting families of their own, and sometimes (albeit more rarely) they would establish businesses of their own.[18] Harder to trace are their informal apprenticeships (since there would be no written contract), but it seems that for centuries girls often were trained (in sewing, for instance) by people outside of their immediate families. It is also clear that there was an increase in formal female apprenticeships in the seventeenth and eighteenth centuries, especially in England. It may be that the social unrest and political changes of this period created more space for women and girls to maneuver in what has been called the

—

"Industrious Revolution."[19] Whereas the Industrial Revolution was controlled by men and is linked with the development of cities and of factory work, the Industrious Revolution refers to the myriad ways that domestic labor increased in scale through new networks in response to increased societal demands.

One of those who took advantage of this space was Eleanor Mosley. Her story—and that of other female apprentices in eighteenth-century England—is told by the economic and social historian Amy Louise Erickson.[20] Eleanor was bound to a milliner, George Tyler, and his wife Lucy. The Tylers already had other young women apprentices, and Eleanor joined a program of training that would allow her eventually to ply her trade in London. It took her eight years to "take the freedom" and become a full member of the Clockmakers Company, which had jurisdiction over this work. Soon she brought her own apprentices to train with her in her own shop. The first was her younger sister, Catherine, and within a month she had added the daughter of a clergyman. She ran her business for at least fifteen years, and she married in her mid-forties. Milliners before the seventeenth century were mostly men, but by the time Eleanor was bound apprentice many girls had learned this trade as a means of gaining some independence in a changing world. Erickson relates the stories of several women who continued to be successful entrepreneurs after they married. Although girls were usually denied formal schooling, the apprenticeship system could at times allow them to thrive as students. "The parents of millinery apprentices took a risk in sending their daughters to the capital for seven years in their teens," Erickson writes. "But it was a calculated risk, and one that many parents thought worth the gain for their daughters and themselves. These girls were apprenticed to milliners by their parents with every intention of ensuring that they made a 'career' for themselves — not in the professional structure, from which they were barred, but as entrepreneurs."[21]

Not all — women or men — succeeded as apprentices. Failure was fairly likely, and after escaping from their trade "bondage" these young people had to find other ways to keep learning how to get along on their own in society. In the 1700s the apprentice system was under pressure from cultural and economic shifts, and the number of young people who fulfilled their full term declined. Let's look now at two famously failed apprentices in the eighteenth century who went on to do extraordinary things: Jean-Jacques Rousseau in Geneva and Benjamin Franklin in Boston. Geneva was a republic in theory run by its male citizens, those who were regarded by law as independent and free. In fact, the republic had a powerful class system, and breaking the hierarchy usually came at a steep price. Craftsmen made up the bulk of the Rousseau family — generations of watchmakers who were highly skilled and active in the city's public life. Jean-Jacques's father married an upper-class woman; both were educated and valued broad literacy. As the philosopher would say many years later, a watchmaker in France knew how to talk about watches; a watchmaker in Geneva could discuss anything with anyone.[22]

But Jean-Jacques did not enter the family trade. His mother died shortly after giving birth to him, and some years later his father had a dispute with the authorities that led him to leave the city. Rousseau was placed with an uncle who tried to attach him to a clerk, and, when that failed, to an engraver. Rousseau was "bound" to a M. Ducommun, a young master metal engraver "of a very violent and boorish character" who ran his shop with a firm hand.

Jean-Jacques was an unusual young man in many respects. He possessed an uncommonly strong independent streak, and he was very proud of having had an education in Latin with a strong tilt toward Roman history. Ducommun saw it as his task to knock this highfalutin distracting stuffing out of the would-be engraver's head. Rousseau learned all too well that the place of the apprentice in the hierarchy could be brutally enforced: "Such was the tyranny of my master that, in the end, work that I would otherwise have liked became intolerable, and I acquired vices that I would have otherwise have hated, such as lying, laziness and stealing. Perpetually shackled to my work, I saw nothing but objects of pleasure to others and of privation to me alone. . . . In a word, everything I saw became an object of desire, for no other reason than because I was not permitted to enjoy anything."[23]

Rousseau goes on to describe how he stole from others on behalf of one journeyman, and then stole from him. For the troubled apprentice, learning how to fool the master became more interesting than learning the skills of his craft. He was punished, of course, but this did not have the desired effect: "I had soon endured so many beatings that I became less fearful; I saw in them . . . compensation for what I stole, which gave me the right to go on doing it. Instead of looking backwards and thinking of the punishment, I looked ahead and thought only of revenge."[24]

In his time off, Jean-Jacques would often take long walks in the countryside with friends, and if they were not back to the gates of the city on time, they would find themselves locked out for the night. This would result in receiving a serious beating from his master, and on one such occasion he determined to run away. At fifteen he left his native city for good, though he professed a lifelong respect for its civic institutions and customs. He even thought that the apprenticeship system might have served him well had he not had the misfortune of being bound to a tyrannical master whose mistreatment rendered him "unsociable." Looking back on this tortured period in his life, Rousseau dreamed of what might have been had his master been a better teacher who made him a better student: "Nothing would have been more congenial to my temperament nor more conducive to my happiness than the peaceful and obscure condition of a good artisan, especially one belonging to as respected a class as the engravers in Geneva."[25]

The apprenticeship system was exported from Europe to its far-flung settlements around the globe. The Franklin family had settled in the rapidly expanding Massachusetts colony, and this was where Benjamin would grow up. His father had a large family to support, but young Ben was a strong reader, and they both thought he might enter the church or even become a scholar. But this plan turned out to be too expensive, and by age ten Ben was trimming wicks and helping his father with candle making. The young man dreamed of going to sea, but an older sibling had drowned so the family wouldn't hear of it. For two years Ben helped his father, who also introduced the boy to a variety of trades to see if there might be one more to his liking than candle making. But some of the apprentice agreements required significant payments, and the Franklins had many mouths to feed. When an older son, James, returned from England and set up a printer's shop in Boston, the family agreed that Benjamin, age twelve, would be bound an apprentice to James for nine years. At least Ben could use his reading skills as he learned to set type.

And indeed, those literary skills did come in handy, even leading the young man to compose ballads. Dissuaded from poetry by his very utilitarian father, Ben took to improving his prose writing, succeeding in placing some columns anonymously in his brother's newspaper. Eventually found out, the apprentice did not receive the applause he expected from James. "Though a brother, he considered himself as my master, and me as his apprentice, and, accordingly, expected the same services from me as he would from another, while I thought he demean'd me too much in some he requir'd of me, who from a brother expected more indulgence." Although Ben's work afforded him ample time to expand his knowledge and improve his writing skills, the hierarchy that was part of both family and the apprenticeship began to weigh on him: "My brother was passionate, and had often beaten me, which I took extremely amiss; and, thinking my apprenticeship very tedious, I was continually wishing for some opportunity of shortening it, which at length offered in a manner unexpected."[26]

The "manner unexpected" came when James, having run afoul of the authorities for publishing scandalous material, was imprisoned and banned from publishing his newspaper. Ben was formally released from his apprenticeship so that he could be named the paper's publisher, thus evading the sanction on James. A private contract was created to keep the younger brother bound in service, but when a dispute arose, Ben decided to break it. The industrious young man had learned a trade and now wanted to practice it on his own. He had also learned how difficult it was to enforce a conflict outside the public sphere! The student already felt quite independent, ready to break free of the teacher, but in order to do so he had to leave Boston. Ben Franklin went on to establish himself as a printer in Philadelphia, and the rest, as they say, is history.

Rousseau and Franklin learned different things from their failed apprenticeships. Both made use of their critical intelligence to undermine the legitimacy of those who were supposed to be their superiors. Like Socrates' interlocutors, Rousseau and Franklin examined the moral basis of their societies' hierarchies, and they found no legitimate basis for the authority to which they were subject. These apprentices became students in a much broader sense. The philosopher from Geneva learned very little about engraving, but he took away profound lessons about a love of equality and a hatred of tyranny. The more he felt oppressed, the more he valued gaining independence. Rousseau also looked back on his experience of being bound to a master as a time of corruption — a time when he became a student of dishonesty, resentment, and anger — and he would try to unlearn those lessons for the rest of his life. Franklin, too, learned to appreciate independence as he bridled under the authority of his "passionate" older brother, but he always valued the other lessons learned while practicing a skill. When he published his own newspaper in Philadelphia, he drew on both his mechanical understanding of printing and his keen sense of what readers were looking for in a regular news bulletin. His love of reading and study would lead him to publish Cicero's *Cato Major,* a discourse on old age that he printed in especially large letters so that "the *Pain* small Letters give the Eyes" would not in the least diminish "the *Pleasure* of the Mind."[27] Long after he set type to earn a living, Franklin appreciated the habits he'd acquired as a student of printing who made that trade his own. These were habits that translated well into many other facets of his life.

Students absorb so much beyond what their instructors believe they are teaching. In premodern rural Europe, children learned informally how to contribute to their households, often by imitating their elders. Apprentices formally learned a specific set of skills and practices, but they also picked up on their societies' hierarchies, values, and customs. Long before formal apprenticeships were common, a large part of being a student was being inculcated with habits that preserve social continuity, though sometimes failure to follow the rules led to innovation.

In addition to these informal modes of learning, a tiny minority of children attended schools in which they received regular instruction from teachers, often in church settings. Looking back centuries before Rousseau and Franklin, we can see that Christianity was a religion grounded in texts, but only a small percentage of the population could read. Still, some young people were trained to recite Latin, to participate in prayer, and to understand the core tenets of the religion. And as religion became a contested terrain after the Reformation, and as social and economic networks grew more complex, the advantages of literacy and of a formal education grew more apparent.

In medieval Christian Europe babies were baptized the day after birth to ensure salvation at a time when infant mortality was high. Very young children were not required to go to church, though they might be taught a few prayers by godparents or parents. Although the peasantry was still by and large illiterate in the 1300s, everyone's life was affected by texts. Whether it was public readings of Scripture or official documents recording sales, births, or deaths, the written word was becoming an ever-greater part of common life.[28] Wealthier families especially needed to read, engage with, and sometimes create texts, and their heads of households increasingly recognized literacy as a core component of prosperity. They sent their male children to school.

In medieval England, elementary education (often in "song schools" in which one learned to chant prayers) was focused on learning the alphabet and on the recitation and reading of Latin.

Clergy, but also sometimes clerks and others who had facility with the written word, would instruct male students in reading and pronunciation, for there was no silent reading until much later in the early modern period. Those few girls who knew Latin learned it at home. In the schools, a handful of poems, meant to deliver moral and life lessons, were taught aside from the sacred texts. These were instructions for the elite. The vast majority of people didn't have the time or the money to enroll their sons in schools of any sort. As literacy slowly increased and paper was introduced in the 1300s, the benefits became clearer of having someone in the family capable of reading. Schools became more popular, starting in cities and spreading to larger towns.

During the Renaissance, many schools went beyond the teaching of Latin and sacred texts. The high points of secular tradition, not just religion, were thought to enrich a student's life. The glories of the ancient world were worthwhile in themselves. Boys in Italy in the 1400s might be given Caesar's commentaries to study in addition to the Vulgate (St. Jerome's translation of the Bible into Latin). They might also encounter Virgil's *Aeneid* or the speeches of Cicero — offered as complex works of literature instructive in the subtleties of history and politics. Ovid's *Metamorphoses* was a basic reading for many young men. During the Renaissance, Greek texts also entered the syllabus as teachers came to recognize how much their Roman heroes depended on Greek predecessors. Science had a place in the curriculum, too, though mostly because teachers knew that the ancients they admired had themselves been interested in scientific inquiry. So too mathematics, though teachers and students certainly also saw the usefulness of arithmetic in an increasingly commercial society, and of geometry in cities planning to expand. The study of the heavens wasn't just the contemplation of angels

---

and saints for Renaissance students. In schools, astronomy was coming into its own at the expense of astrology. A student in a Renaissance school expected more than literacy and more than discipline and the rigors of religion. He expected to become well rounded through education, and this meant becoming capable of living a cultivated, fully human life. This notion of liberal learning harkened back to the ancient world and a mode of education whose goal was not narrowly instrumental but broadly connected to the virtues and the capacities of the whole person. Devotion to God might be part of that, to be sure, and you might also learn things that you could use in public or private life. But the Renaissance student was being turned toward the goal of continual cultivation, a more secular goal for living well in this life rather than preparing for one's just reward in the next.

The Protestant Reformation, too, contributed to a broadening of what a student might learn. Biblical literacy was important for Protestants wanting to experience the word of God directly, and this — together with the invention in Europe of the printing press in the mid-fifteenth century — led over time to increased literacy. Schools became ever more important, and not just for reproducing the clergy and other elites. Teaching was becoming a profession of its own. "If God chose to keep me away from pastoral functions," Martin Luther said in one of his 1540 Table Talks, "there is no other occupation I would more gladly take up than schoolmaster, for next to the pastor's work, no other is more beautiful or significant than this."[29] He went on to say that we can do without princes, nobles, and mayors, but we can't do without schoolteachers. Luther argued that schooling was too important to leave to families, and in the wake of his religious teaching one sees an increase in the number of charters granted to schools in German-speaking Europe.[30] The call of Jesus – "Follow me!" – was to be taken to heart by Protestants who longed for spiritual rebirth, and an education often seemed helpful to young souls who were open to this appeal. After the Protestants came to power in Geneva, they made schooling compulsory – for boys and even for girls! Who could be a student was changing. John Calvin had a universal mission and intense civic duties, but he found time for curriculum development as a vehicle for spreading access to the Good News. Catholic authorities countered by developing their own schools to defend the faith against the Protestant heresy, keep students within the Church, and provide them with the necessary tools to lead properly Christian lives. Education wasn't only about religion, but the two would remain closely intertwined until waves of secularization hit the West in the latter half of the eighteenth century.

The sunny Protestant view of every child as a potential student had a dark undercurrent. Pre-Reformation educators saw young people as malleable wax in need of being formed. They believed that a particular body of appropriate knowledge would form students to fit within a given community. It wasn't just acquiring facts that mattered, but harmonious integration. Many post-Reformation thinkers, by contrast, viewed education as a tool to break the young and separate them from their evil inclinations. Especially for Calvinists and some evangelical Protestants, children were creatures of appetite, and appetites were evil. "Break their will that you may save their souls," counseled the evangelist John Wesley.[31] Sure, you had to teach the little ones to read, but these students had to read in order to separate themselves from their natural inclinations.

From the religious perspective, education was to steer the student away from evil, a challenging task because evil was embedded in the student's very nature. You became "independent" from sinful instincts so that you might be saved. If you were going to follow Jesus, you had, to use modern parlance, to unfollow your appetites. From a more secular perspective, education was to lead you toward economic independence and participation in the life of the community. On the one hand, students in early modern Europe were supposed to learn the skills to be autonomous enough to leave their parents' household. On the other hand, education was supposed to inculcate in you the mores of your parents; students might leave the household of their birth, but they must take the customs and conventions of that household with them when they go.

Thus, by the seventeenth century in Europe, an education was increasingly important for both the religious and secular dimensions of life. Participation in one's church community was progressively more textually based. Churches were employers and to get a job one often needed to be able to read the Bible, engage with its principal commentators, and skillfully stay on the right side of the ecclesiastic authorities in one's region. In commerce and civil society, literacy and basic arithmetic skills were real advantages as trade increased and formal contracts became commonplace. If you were fortunate enough to go beyond the basic schooling offered in the village, you could learn skills that would help you navigate a changing world. Those with arithmetic skills could find work in commerce, and as commerce grew so did the need for those who could help settle legal matters. An understanding of contracts and the ability to negotiate details might lead one to a career in the legal or civic sphere. However much you learned, though, you were also expected not to change the status quo too much. Although there are plenty of reports of young people causing a ruckus, the well-educated student, however rare, was meant to fit in.

———

Students in the seventeenth century were sometimes seen as blank slates on which the teacher could write, and sometimes as fertile fields in which the teacher would sow seeds of knowledge. Both metaphors, despite worries about sinful appetites, reflected optimistic aspects of the humanism that emerged from the Renaissance. Students, especially boys from well-to-do families, were learning to become independent from their families in the present by drawing on the resources found in the legacies of great thinkers of the past. Learning to adapt those legacies would help lead to a fulfilling life, but it was also thought that students needed to internalize authority because of their own sinful natures. Students would be "independent" only when they learned to obey the powers that they had made their own. One might follow Jesus in one's spiritual life, but in public students were meant to be less Socratic gadflies than Confucian harmonizers. The good student was one who didn't need an outside master saying what to do because the "inside master" guided behavior. The philosopher John Locke put it succinctly in his *Treatise on Education:* "All virtue and excellency lies in a power of denying ourselves the satisfaction of our own desires where reason does not authorize them."[32] For Locke and for many thinkers in the wake of the Reformation, teachers began controlling students in ways that would eventually lead those students to control themselves, despite their sinful inclinations.

Control isn't the first thing that comes to mind in thinking about the students at the first universities, which developed out of monasteries and cathedral schools in the twelfth century. Those universities were not intentional creations; groups of scholars and clerics studying together at some point just started using the word *universitas* as a label for their endeavors. Sometimes it was a charismatic teacher who gathered young men around him – like Peter Abelard, who around 1100 created a "school" near Paris to continue his approach to theology. Sometimes a city attracted educated people who trained others for work in a growing urban environment. Teaching and studying took place in Bologna for decades before a "university" there was formally recognized by the pope in 1291. In many ways the university was like other guilds in that it licensed its members as apprentices (students), and masters (professors). Universities controlled their own finances and had legal autonomy through the appropriate monarchical authorities. Over time, municipal and ecclesiastical authorities gave students and teachers a variety of privileges to protect their educational efforts. There were stipends for some, and for others exemptions from military duty or other civic responsibilities. Those in search of an education often came to the university from a great distance, and when they completed a course of study, the recognition of that completion, a diploma, would be accepted by other institutions. This helped universalize the university. Although the lingua franca was Latin, the larger schools organized themselves into "nations," groups of faculty members who hailed from one part of Europe or another. By the thirteenth century, Bologna and Montpellier stood out as the important universities in the south – and Paris and Oxford in the north. Amazingly, eighteen universities founded in the twelfth century still exist today![33]

A student who wanted to attend a university in the twelfth to thirteenth centuries would not have been looking for a campus. He would have been looking for a scholar – a master who would take him on as a student and explain what he needed to learn. Within a hundred years or so, distinctive residential environments would evolve in which a teacher/master would also oversee a student's living arrangements. Libraries and attractive quads were built too. By the 1400s, a university was a physical place as well as a center of learning. The students who came to Bologna or Oxford in the 1400s were aiming to enter the Church. Some of them were younger sons of nobility with titles but no inheritance. Others were coming from large towns where they had excelled in the local school and saw a career in the Church as the best vehicle for advancement. Even early on, there were some provisions made for poor students – forgoing fees, perhaps, or simply allowing them to beg.

The students at these early universities quickly earned reputations for less than pious behavior. Even in the earliest days, there was a proliferation of disciplinary rules as schools sought to curb the rambunctious, sometimes violent behavior of their students. Popes issued edicts emphasizing that you were a real student only if you were assigned to a master/teacher, and that this teacher could be held accountable for your behavior. They also urged students to refrain from going about the town with their swords! Over time, school administrators issued warnings about gambling, swearing oaths, frequenting brothels, and much else.[34]

Key to being a member of the university was fluency in Latin. Students could be required to speak Latin in all conversations, even with other students. The records are full of reported violations of these rules. Latin enabled the student to study theology and participate in religious ceremonies, and it announced that he was a "university man" – a member of a very particular guild. Sometimes students tried to signal their identity with distinctive clothing, but this could be frowned upon by professors who expected "approved mediocrity" in dress. Students themselves developed their own signs and rituals of belonging, and like fraternity practices of the modern era, these often involved hazing. First-year students were objects of physical abuse, forced confessions, and the levying of heavy fees to pay for the banquets of more senior students. Over time, professors and administrative authorities attempted to protect freshmen and thereby secure their own authority over the scholarly and residential enterprise. Discipline meted out by the schools could be simple fines, but some universities even had their own jails. The tension between the authority wielded by organized students and that exercised by organized professors (and later administrators) is, indeed, an old story.

Students at Bologna or Paris pursued an education in the liberal arts, which was called the *trivium* or the *quadrivium*. The trivium was made up of the verbal disciplines of grammar, rhetoric, and logic, and the quadrivium was oriented to the more quantitative fields of arithmetic, geometry, music, and astronomy. The universities of Italy and southern France tended to emphasize the verbal fields, while the more quantitative areas were given prominence in universities to the north. Students competed with one another for their master's approval and for coveted Church positions upon completing their studies. Students attended early-morning lectures in which they memorized the interpretations of canonical texts offered by their teachers and practiced their own argumentation later in the day. Professors who spoke too quickly during their lectures might find themselves not just the object of ridicule but also the target of rocks thrown by auditors trying to memorize what they were hearing. For their part, professors gave examinations that could be brutally hard. Often the student had to argue for and against a canonical question. How does Aristotle compare with the Bible on the question of free will? On the definition of happiness? Progress was measured by how successfully the student argued without straying into heresy or licentious areas. Verbal fencing was high stakes since the most adept would secure real vocational benefits.

—

Like the apprentice who became a master, a university student who was successful and moved from undergraduate memorization to advanced disputation might himself become a professor. It would be possible, say, to specialize in the law and then begin teaching future clerks or advocates. But students did not earn such positions because of doing original work. Universities before the modern era were not centers of research. Their function was not to create new knowledge but to disseminate the truths that religion and society held as foundational. Students became teachers by showing they had a secure grasp of those foundations. Although through their studies they may have aimed at financial independence, they were nonetheless also followers.

In all the examples of being a student we have discussed thus far, we see the development of different kinds of agency. In the West before the modern age, students, whether working on domestic chores at home, apprenticing with a skilled tradesperson in a town, or studying with a learned theologian in a city, were developing their capacities for purposeful independence. That independence was fundamentally economic, but it was always in relation to a broader culture; part of learning was coming to terms with the possibilities and limits of independence. Students were not just repeating prayers or acquiring skills; they were still figuring out how they might stand on their own feet and how they might stand in relation to others.

But not every person could be a student. As Europeans explored the world and created colonies far from their native lands, they also created a new class of people who lived among them but did not count as fellow subjects, let alone as friends or neighbors. Slaves, mostly from Africa, were used to build new societies or shore up old economies, and by the 1700s there were millions of Africans who had been forcibly taken from their homes and coerced into labor around the world. Some countries, like France, had long outlawed the practice of human bondage. If you set foot on French soil, you were supposed to be free. But the money made from African labor meant that laws would be reconfigured, and the question of who was really "human" would arise for those who aimed to justify the profitable oppression. This also meant reimagining what it meant to learn and to be a student. The Africans who survived the horrific journey across the ocean received brutal lessons about authority, violence, and power. Survival required learning these lessons well, but it would be perverse to describe this as being a student. What, then, can be said? What did it mean for a slave to learn in the Americas in a situation of brutally violent hierarchy? Philosophers chimed in to claim that Africans were biologically so different from Europeans that they were incapable of the kind of learning that resulted in the independence at which students aimed. Henry Louis Gates Jr. has for many years written about how the Enlightenment's emphasis on the faculty of reason was joined to racist prejudice to deny that newly "discovered" races were fully human. David Hume, for example, would claim there were "no arts, no sciences" on the African continent.[35] Its inhabitants were not capable of thinking freely. But slaves did receive an education in labor — whether that was in mines, fields, or in the master's house. Slaves were often meant to become skillful, and their skills could be highly valued by those who wanted to keep them in bondage. But in the cultural economy of slavery, the slaves were not to be "educated," not to be treated as "students" — for the student is expected at some point to graduate, and graduation is associated with independence. In some of the North American colonies, it was specifically against the law to teach slaves to read. South Carolina, for example, passed a law in 1740 that fined anyone caught helping a slave become literate. Almost a century later, North Carolina instituted a law indicating that "any free person, who shall hereafter teach, or attempt to teach, any slave within this State to read or write, the use of figures excepted, or shall give or sell to such slave or slaves any books or pamphlets, shall be liable to indictment in any court of record in this State."[36] And throughout this period in the South, those spurred by religious fervor to introduce blacks to the Bible faced the wrath of communities dedicated more to white supremacy than to the salvation of souls.

In the rare event that the slaveholder did, in fact, offer an education to a slave, the cognitive tension of maintaining a person's status as property while also treating that person as a student could grow into felt contradiction. The experience of Phillis Wheatley Peters, the first African American to publish a book of poetry, is revealing. Kidnapped at about age seven in West Africa and shipped to Boston in 1761, she was deemed on arrival too weak for the manual work expected of child slaves. The Wheatley family was "in want of a domestic" but quickly saw that this sickly child was remarkably precocious. Phillis was introduced to the Greek and Latin classics by the adult children in the household, who also acquainted her with the literature and science of the day. Before long, the young slave was composing her own verses, and one of her first poems was a paean to those fortunate enough to study at a university:

> Students, to you 'tis giv'n to scan the heights
> Above, to traverse the ethereal space,
> And mark the systems of revolving worlds.

The enslaved girl urges privileged university students to resist temptation and instead follow their appetite for learning:

Ye blooming plants of human race divine,
An *Ethiop* tells you 'tis your greatest foe;
Its transient sweetness turns to endless pain,
And in immense perdition sinks the soul.

"To the University of Cambridge, in New-England" is thought to be Peters's first poem, although it was not published until 1773. She is now considered to have written more than one hundred, and while most of her subjects were religious, she also wrote about the colonies' struggle with England for independence. A poem written in 1778 to honor General Wooster reminded her readers that the struggle for freedom remained terribly inconsistent:

With thine own hand conduct them and defend
And bring the dreadful contest to an end —
For ever grateful let them live to thee
And keep them ever Virtuous, brave, and free —
But how, presumtuous shall we hope to find
Divine acceptance with th' Almighty mind —
While yet (O deed Ungenerous!) they disgrace
And hold in bondage Afric's blameless race?
Let Virtue reign — And thou accord our prayers
Be victory our's, and generous freedom theirs.[37]

The Wheatley household saw in Phillis a prodigy, and she was educated in literature and history as she continued to write her own verses. She had some access to a world that prized freedom and redemption, and in 1774, having already been celebrated for her learning in London and in New England, the poet was finally manumitted. Around this time, she wrote to the Reverend Samson Occum: "In every human

Breast, God has implanted a Principle, which we call Love of freedom; it is impatient of Oppression, and pants for Deliverance; and by the Leave of our modern Egyptians I will assert that the same Principle lives in us." The contradiction in American belief between the rhetoric of freedom and the oppression of slavery was all too evident to Peters: "To convince them of the strange Absurdity of their Conduct whose Words and Actions are so diametrically, opposite, I humbly think it does not require the Penetration of a Philosopher to determine."[38]

To be accepted as a student meant to be accepted as a human being who was learning to choose a future. Learning inspired a taste for freedom. So slaves could not be students; students could not be slaves. This was the lesson learned by the brilliant Frederick Douglass in the mid-1800s. Having suffered greatly as a slave child in rural Maryland, he found affection and comfort when he was moved to Baltimore at around age ten. There, under the gentle care of the pious Sophia Auld, a young woman not yet used to owning other human beings, the young slave learned to read the Bible. In the beginning, he would listen to her recite from the book of Job as he lay pretending to sleep under the table at her feet! He was learning to read the Bible on his own when Sophia's husband returned to Baltimore to remind her that teaching slaves to read was illegal in Maryland. Reading would make the boy "forever unfit" to fulfill the duties of a slave, he told her, and there "would be no keeping him." Douglass never forgot those words. Later, having escaped slavery and become a famous abolitionist, he returned to them again and again in his books and speeches. The stern slaveholder Master Auld criticizing his wife for treating the slave as a student, he decided, was the first antislavery lecture he had ever heard: "Very well, thought I. Knowledge unfits a child to be a slave. I instinctively assented to the proposition, and from that moment I understood the direct pathway from slavery to freedom."[39]

During the long years of slavery, Africans found ways to teach one another even in the bleakest of conditions. So-called pit schools, for example, were places far from the overseer's gaze where slaves could teach one another reading and writing skills with whatever implements they could find.[40] In her *Incidents in the Life of a Slave Girl*, the former slave and pioneering educator Harriet Jacobs underscored that the battle over learning was a conflict regarding what it could mean to be free. She gave harrowing accounts of white militias going through slave quarters looking for signs of literacy. "Since many slaveholders believed that slave literacy begat slave insurrection, the only proof needed to condemn a slave was provocatively written materials." When Jacobs escaped from slavery, she continued to view education as the path to freedom. "The more my mind was enlightened," she wrote, "the more difficult it was for me to consider myself an article for property."[41] In her *Incidents* she related her sacrifices to ensure that her own children could be students so that they could leave slavery behind. And she founded the Jacobs Free School in Virginia to provide a path to authentic freedom through learning to blacks who had been forbidden to pursue an education. At the free school, black teachers taught black students, learning together, Jacobs hoped, how to become full citizens of a nation that had for centuries denied their very humanity by depriving them of access to knowledge.

The direct pathway to freedom was education, and nothing made that more apparent than attempts to block it. Freedom here meant much more than economic independence; it signified being recognized fully as a human being. For Douglass, the arc of his own life exemplified the link between learning and freedom. He knew that in the context of enforced white supremacy, learning to read was "running away with myself."[42] In a powerful 1852 speech denouncing America's celebrations of the Fourth of July, he pointed out the national hypocrisy in celebrating freedom while defending slavery. Those who fell back on talk of the natural supremacy of white people were even more base in their duplicity because of their efforts to keep black people from having access to an education. The obvious fact that slaves could learn exposed the rhetoric of freedom celebrated by white supremacists as especially hollow even as it made the slave's humanity painfully visible. Slaves had to be prevented from becoming students in order to keep them oppressed; indeed, laws against teaching slaves existed exactly because their very educability was testimony to their rights to equality and freedom. "It is admitted in the fact that Southern statute books are covered with enactments, forbidding, under severe fines and penalties, the teaching of the slave to read and write. When you can point to any such laws in reference to the beasts of the field," Douglass admonished, "then I may consent to argue the manhood of the slave."[43] As a young slave, Douglass had experienced the epiphany of education: by learning to learn he was already acquiring freedom. State legislatures in the South recognized this as well and through vicious subjugation were determined to prevent education from spreading. States in the North had more subtle mechanisms for this.

Only violence could maintain a system built on the labor of millions who were forcibly denied the opportunity to learn. At the dawn of modernity in the West, the links between education and freedom were underscored by a range of thinkers who began to see students as more than potential disseminators of doctrines and more than imitators of skillful masters. It would take centuries before this idea of the student would be accepted as something that should spread across all categories of gender, class, race, and ethnicity, but eventually the demand to learn, *the right to be a student,* would reach far and wide across the globe.

Chapter 3

THE EMERGENCE OF THE MODERN STUDENT

"Enlightenment is man's emergence from his self-incurred immaturity." This ringing first sentence of Kant's 1784 essay "What Is Enlightenment?" signals the arrival of the modern notion of the student. Enlightenment is, for Kant, the process of learning, and that process aims at liberating one from "tutelage." Enlightenment allows one to grow up, to reach the age of responsibility, without which one suffers from an "inability to use one's own understanding without the guidance of another." Beginning in the late eighteenth century the student increasingly becomes someone in the process of enlightenment. This idea is new. It means that students are to use their own understanding rather than depend on authorities to guide them. Just as we mature physically, crawling and then walking on our own, we mature mentally and become capable of thinking on our own. Or we should become so capable. Fear held many back, Kant believed, which is why he linked enlightenment to daring: "Sapere aude! Have courage to use your own reason!" – "that is the motto of enlightenment," he wrote.[1]

At the time Kant wrote his essay, the Enlightenment was already regarded as a transformative intellectual/cultural movement. Science and mathematics had been making significant advances since the late seventeenth century, and many expected advances to continue in ways that would radically alter society. As change in the world accelerated, the role of tradition weakened. This, of course, didn't happen everywhere and it didn't happen all at once, but we see beliefs increasingly being justified with arguments and evidence rather than with appeals to authority or to "It goes without saying." Historians refer to a low and a high Enlightenment, by which they mean cultural movements of the street and those of literate society. The former can be seen in gossip, lewd pamphlets, and even far-fetched conspiracy theories that made people increasingly skeptical of those in authority, the latter in philosophical debates that showed why skepticism was an intellectual position worth arguing about. Kant, no ally of the skeptic, nevertheless acknowledged and applauded the ethos of questioning all: "Our age is the age of criticism, to which everything must submit. Religion through its holiness and legislation through its majesty commonly seek to exempt themselves from it. But in this way they excite a just suspicion against themselves, and cannot lay claim to that unfeigned respect that reason grants only to that which has been able to withstand its free and public examination." Free and public examination and the courage to use one's own reason would, Kant thought, lead inevitably to progress. As people grew accustomed to thinking for themselves and discussing their concerns in public, they would become more reasonable, more prudent: "For enlightenment of this kind, all that is needed is freedom," Kant wrote. "And the freedom in question is the most innocuous form of all — freedom to make public use of one's reason in all matters."[2] When the public becomes collectively able to think for itself, revolution is avoided and deliberative change is possible. With freedom we can be students, and as students, we expand the realm of freedom.

Kant was mainly concerned with the student writ large — society in the process of enlightenment — rather than with individual students in schools. During his lifetime, though, a new ethos of teaching and learning was taking root around him in Prussia. There was more training for teachers and, eventually, compulsory primary school for all young people. Kant himself was the child of a master harness maker, and he went to school in Königsburg (then in Prussia, now in Russia). In the early grades of such schools, a sole teacher would give instruction in reading, writing, arithmetic, and Christianity, which would be followed by more rigorous training. As a university student, the future philosopher studied Latin every semester, and he also learned Greek, Hebrew, and French. Science and mathematics entered the curriculum later, with philosophy introduced in the semesters before graduation. Kant's school was Pietistic, which meant that students were expected to experience strong religious emotions, although Kant himself is said to have preferred the study of classical texts to the expression of spiritual enthusiasm. In eighteenth-century Europe much of education still entailed memorization, learning to recite texts or recopy them. Learning was largely regurgitation. The notion of education articulated in "What Is Enlightenment?" was aspirational — and a reaction against the author's own experience as a student. Later in life, Kant acknowledged that he would be overcome by "terror and apprehension" whenever he thought back on "the slavery" of his youth.[3]

Few students in the eighteenth century would have associated school with learning to think for themselves. There were certainly changes in the curriculum in many parts of Europe, especially in the latter part of the century, but an emphasis on Latin and rote exercises was still common. The point of such exercises wasn't just to improve literacy or become familiar with rituals. As we saw in the previous chapter, the philosopher John Locke, writing in England at the very end of the 1600s, argued that the natural inclinations of students needed to be disciplined so as to direct their passions to virtuous ends. Custom and habit should shape passions, and ideas introduced to students should help them be productive in society. Locke famously speculated that minds began as blank slates, but when it came to interactions with others, he believed that base instincts were always already in play – and that people had to learn not to satisfy them. Schooling had much to do with disciplining those instincts. In Catholic France the theological armature was different, but the gist of the story was much the same: natural inclinations were evil, and education disciplined one against satisfying them. An important figure in the educational circles of the early 1700s was Charles Rollin, a rector at the Sorbonne inclined toward the Augustinian dimension of Catholicism known as Jansenism. Rollin emphasized the downright sinful nature of the unchecked passions and the importance of educating the child to prevent those passions from being acted upon. For Rollin, the key to such education was religion. The structures of religion were the same as the structures of society, and the task of education was to ensure that the young person could successfully assimilate to them. These structures, the mores of a society, were not just convention; they reflected the divine plan for creation: "These rules and laws [of existing morality] are not arbitrary and dependent upon the fancies of men; they are imprinted in the substance of the soul, by the creator; they exist before all ages, and are of greater antiquity than the world, as they are an emanation of the divine wisdom, which cannot think otherwise of virtue and vice."[4] Rollin wanted students to understand their obligation to the existing order as they would understand their obligation to God, for then they would be moved to fall in with that order rather than with their natural (sinful) inclinations.

Although Rollin would be forced out of positions of authority because of his Jansenist views, his influence on educational thinking was powerful both in his country and in the Protestant-dominated colonies of North America. Indeed, translations of Rollin's works were as likely to be found in American houses as a Bible or Milton's *Paradise Lost*. While Rollin's *Traité des études* was an important contribution to the theory of education, what made the most educational impact in America was his broad history of antiquity. A popular genre of the times was "universal history," novelistic accounts of the broad sweep of human development from the earliest known civilizations to the contemporary period. Rollin's history began with the biblical account of creation and worked its way up to the Egyptians, Carthaginians, Assyrians, Babylonians, Medes, and Persians. As one might expect, the Greco-Roman world featured prominently. Like many writers of universal history, Rollin sought to instruct readers in moral lessons that would serve them and their societies well. Exemplars were key. The Romans of the Republic thought of the public good first and were ready to sacrifice self-interest on behalf of the whole. As Charles Salas has put it, "Rollin saw strengthening one's resistance to evil as the main purpose of education, and he made every effort to make his young readers feel admiration for Roman virtues; it was an education of the heart he was after more than the education of the mind. His history must impart 'the principles of religion and true piety'; it must make students 'good sons, good masters, good friends, good citizens'; and it must make them fit for polite society – 'learned, skillful, eloquent and capable of adapting to any career.'" Rollin told a historical tale that underscored the virtues of the liberally educated Greeks and Romans, especially in contrast to the Carthaginians, whose education was confined to commerce and self-interest, resulting in narrow-mindedness and corruption. No friend of democracy, Rollin was impressed by the Senate of Republican Rome which, "guided by the prudence of old men, could not fail of prevailing over a state [Carthage] which was governed wholly by the giddy multitude." The lessons of Greece and Rome should move the student away from capriciousness, selfishness, and the passions toward the prudence, virtue, and sacrifice for the common good that reflected the divine plan – as Salas puts it: "to take potential Carthaginians and mold them into Romans."[5]

So the Protestant philosopher (Locke) and the Catholic priest (Rollin) agreed that a primary goal of education was to triumph over self-interest, learning instead to love the common good. Locke looked to education to help the mind control the body. Rollin looked to education to turn students from the selfish pursuit of luxury that "would destroy the most flourishing states and kingdoms."[6] For both thinkers, being a student meant learning how to give up the quest for private pleasure and to contribute to society.

But how to contribute to a society undergoing rapid changes was not always clear. Locke died in 1704 and Rollin in 1741, and they had witnessed transformative changes in the societies around them. What did it mean to contribute to one's society when one lived amidst a revolution, as Locke did in the late 1680s? The existing order was unstable, so learning how to conform to it seemed like a fool's errand. And changes weren't confined to politics and religion. As commercial enterprises grew rapidly, some people were getting rich, and they also argued they were contributing to the common good. Some Enlightenment thinkers argued that by pursuing self-interest one was actually helping one's neighbors. During these times of political, economic, and scientific change, writers on education claimed that the pursuit of individual achievement would, happily, also lead to social progress. Students should be able to discover better ways of living for themselves and their society.

The dissemination of knowledge was a topic of immense interest both to those who, as Kant would later argue, saw this dissemination as part of the slow, steady evolution of a more just world, and to those who thought that sharing information with common people was a prescription for social unrest among the volatile masses. It was in this context that in the 1750s the public intellectuals/philosophers Denis Diderot and Jean le Rond d'Alembert would launch their extraordinary project of collecting and distributing the world of knowledge in a multivolume work organized as a dictionary. With ten volumes of illustrations and twenty-one volumes of text, their *Encyclopédie* contains more than seventy thousand articles written by more than one hundred authors "on subjects ranging from asparagus to zodiac."[7] Denis Diderot, the lead organizer of the project, wrote about ten thousand of the articles himself![8]

The economist and journalist Joachim Faiguet de Villeneuve contributed about a score of entries to the *Encyclopédie* on topics ranging from the sacred to the mathematical. Faiguet wanted to promote efficiencies in commerce while also reducing the clout of ecclesiastic authorities. The head of a boarding school in Paris in the late 1740s, he penned the *Encyclopédie*'s entry "Studies" ("Études"). Faiguet was a sharp critic of the failure of schools to move beyond rote memorization toward a more skill-based curriculum. Students from ages seven to sixteen were primarily taught Latin composition, an educational program that fostered some good habits but had limited practical value. "Is it fair," Faiguet asked, "to sacrifice the best part of the students, and to make them waste the time and expense of their education, to procure in a few subjects the perfection of a talent which is most often useless, and which is hardly ever needed?" For the Encyclopedist, school should prepare students for life not by encouraging imitation of the teacher's words, but by giving them skills that they could use after their formal schooling had ended. "What is education," Faiguet asked, "if not learning what it is necessary to know & practice in the business of life? Now, can this great object be fulfilled by limiting the instruction of young people to the work of themes and verses?" No, he answered, what students need are skills in "Design, Calculation & Writing, Elementary Geometry, Geography, Music, et cetera."[9] In contrast to Rollin, Faiguet would make Carthaginians out of Romans!

The *Encyclopédie*'s entry on learning was written by Diderot himself. "To *study* is to strive to become knowledgeable. To *learn* is to succeed," he wrote.[10] The entire project of the *Encyclopédie* was to help readers learn outside of formal education, to become knowledgeable about the world by becoming students of independent-minded authors who had explored it. These students would, presumably, develop the appetite and the ability to explore the world on their own.

The Encyclopedists contrasted themselves with earlier abstract thinkers who only obscured understanding with their inherited jargon disconnected from experience. In his entry "School, Philosophy of the" d'Alembert put it plainly in describing the legacy of scholasticism as that which "substitutes words for things, and frivolous and ridiculous questions for the grander objects of real Philosophy, that which explains unintelligible things with barbaric terms; that gives birth to or puts in a place of honor universals, categories, predicaments, metaphysical degrees, second intentions, and the horror of nothingness, etc. This philosophy was born of the mind and of ignorance."[11] The "school" d'Alembert had in mind was scholasticism in the Catholic Church, but the *philosophe* had to be cautious. His language here had to get past the French Church's censors, but the message was clear enough to his eighteenth-century readers. Previous thinkers were beholden to religion or to ambiguous universals that tried to explain one mystery with another. Students of the *Encyclopédie* would be inquirers, not believers. Instead of grounding our lives in secure faith, we should embrace doubt, insisted Diderot (with a nod to Descartes): "Having *studied* well means having *learned* to doubt." With this statement, we have moved far from memorization of Latin verses and toward what Kant a generation later would mean by thinking for oneself. As Diderot concluded his entry on learning: "We *learn* by listening; we *instruct* ourselves by asking questions."[12]

The student in the second half of the eighteenth century in western Europe was less an absorber of lessons and more an acquirer of useful skills who could question the world productively. But another idea emerged during this period — one that is connected both to Kant's notion of enlightenment and to later understandings of "child-centered education." The key figure here is Jean-Jacques Rousseau, whom we met as a discontented apprentice in the previous chapter. As a political philosopher and a theorist of education, Rousseau had a profound impact on Enlightenment notions of reason and on later Romantic ideals of natural flourishing. Rousseau was a thinker full of ambivalences and contradictions. His most celebrated work, *The Social Contract*, begins with his most famous sentence: "Men are born free yet are everywhere in chains." He goes on in that work, though, to ask what would make these chains legitimate. He contributed to the *Encyclopédie* even as he questioned the social value of the arts and sciences. Among his most widely read works was a treatise on education, *Emile*. Rousseau's perspective on the child as student was opposed to that of Locke and Rollin; unlike them, Rousseau did not want education to constrain the child's passions. Rousseau thought of the child not as a fount of unruly instincts or sinful desires but as a natural being who could learn to live in harmony with his or her surroundings, provided those surroundings had not been too corrupted. In the preface to *Emile*, he writes that while he recognizes that his own pedagogic methods might not work for everyone, what really matters is that adults observe children more closely. He tells teachers simply to *pay attention* to their students and to try to understand how *they* navigate in the world: "Begin thus by making a more careful study of your pupils, for it is clear that you know nothing about them."[13] When you do get to know them, he insists, you will see that they are naturally good. The task of the educator, then, is to cultivate that inherent goodness and keep children safe as they discover the world around them. Don't give them lessons, and certainly don't ask them to memorize maxims in physics or morality. Instead, let their experience be their guide. Let them learn by encountering the limitations inherent in the world. One can slip on ice, for instance, or fall from a high place and be injured. This might be learning the hard way, but it was preferable to memorizing laws and rules overlaid upon nature by some authority figure.

—

In Rousseau's account, the child should ideally be educated by a tutor in isolation from others at least until puberty. After infancy, even mothers should play a minor role – and fathers no role at all. The wise tutor knows that the presence of others is an invitation to distort oneself in pursuit of recognition, and so students should build up resilience to allow them to maintain their authenticity before entering into social life. Education is meant to protect the young from forces that pull them away from their natural selves and toward approval seeking. Looking around, Rousseau saw that being a student usually depended upon winning the approval of those in authority, and he saw this as a distortion of the student's true self. The task of Rousseau's tutor is to guide the student into relationships with others based on compassion, not competition or vanity. Eventually, the pupil comes to look upon the teacher as an advisor and friend rather than as an authority figure. Having learned from experience, students achieve maturity by realizing that they can think for themselves. It is worth pointing out that Kant was a great admirer of Rousseau.

Emile is, of course, a little boy, and Rousseau's views of education are bound both by his own prejudices and by the gender prejudices of his time. The philosopher does turn his attention to a little girl, Sophie, but she exists mostly to be brought up as a companion to Emile. Girls should be educated for a lifetime of subordination. Whereas the free development of the boy's nature is fundamental, the girl must learn restraint, which produces "a docility which women need all their lives, since they never cease to be subject either to a man or to the judgments of men, and they are never permitted to put themselves above these judgments." The girl learns to triumph, Rousseau argues, through this docility, as her "gentleness" will eventually allow her to control her male companion with sweetness.[14]

Coming of age in mid-eighteenth-century England, writer and philosopher Mary Wollstonecraft was inspired by Rousseau's political writings and his notion that a legitimate law was one that a people created for itself rather than one imposed by a divinely sanctioned monarch. But she objected strongly to his consignment of little girls to an education in subservience. She had, without any doubt, learned the hard way about life and education. She grew up in a household dominated by a violent, alcoholic father, and she had to struggle to learn the skills that helped her escape her surroundings. She first got away by living with female family friends who supported themselves with sewing and needlework. They then set up a school for girls. Teaching gave her an even greater appetite for understanding more about her world. One of the earliest lessons she learned was that schooling was a path to some independence – at least from her father's house and the threat of an arranged marriage. A teacher herself, Wollstonecraft argued that it was sheer prejudice to expect that girls couldn't grow into individuals capable of exercising their own reason. In *A Vindication of the Rights of Woman* (1702) she points out that men (including Rousseau) haven't used *their* own reason to think through the importance of educating boys *and* girls: "The mind must be strong that resolutely forms its own principles; for a kind of intellectual cowardice prevails which makes many men shrink from the task, or only do it by halves." A strong, courageous mind would recognize that all humans deserve "the most perfect education . . . an exercise of the understanding as is best calculated to strengthen the body and form the heart . . . to enable the individual to attain such habits of virtue as will render it independent." Her "habits of virtue" resonates with the classical tradition of Stoicism and with Rousseau's views of education as the drawing out of a child's capacities, except that she wants girls also to "unfold their faculties" and achieve more autonomy: "It is a farce to call any being virtuous whose virtues do not result from the exercise of its own reason. This was Rousseau's opinion respecting men: I extend it to women."[15]

Wollstonecraft emphasized the important influence that a tutor of good judgment and affection — someone like the author — could have on the development of young girls. Even good students needed to learn from an adult with the proper experience that although competition and vanity often drove those around them, they would find virtue through the exercise of reason and compassion. Being an effective tutor was one way for a woman to show that she had been a good student as a girl, but learning wasn't only about good teaching from her perspective. Unlike Rousseau, Wollstonecraft advised that students be educated in groups. She worried less about vanity springing up among them than about the distorting effects that an older teacher might have on the young — forcing them to grow up too quickly. Children should learn to think for themselves instead of just imitating the tutor, and being together enabled them to "open the heart to friendship and confidence, gradually leading to more expansive benevolence."[16] Autonomy within society required the development of inner resources that would give young people the resilience they would need to weather the challenges of life, and this independence was the principal object of education — for boys and girls. Wollstonecraft was only too aware of the criticisms of women and the argument that their imperfections were evidence that a serious education would be wasted on such frivolous creatures. Her response is scathing. She points out that girls are educated to make them subservient, and then they are criticized for navigating in society from a position of enforced weakness. A proper education would allow women to unfold their true capacities. She chastises

Rousseau for being pessimistic about the true possibilities for the enlightenment of men and women, and she dares to imagine an education for both sexes that would lead to freedom and virtue through autonomy.[17] She imagined autonomy beyond the pursuit of individual pleasure, beyond being successful in the marketplace. Like Rousseau, she wanted students to be grounded in a sense of self, a form of authenticity that would keep them from depending on the validation of others. Women had to be enlightened enough to no longer need the approval of those in power. So did men.[18] Students were those who recognized their capacities for "perfectibility," for the development of potential through practices that lead to independence. The same faculties that allow boys and men to become students enable girls and women to do the same.

Are students supposed to mirror society so that they find their traditional place within it? Many philosophers writing on education, including Rousseau and Wollstonecraft, said no, but most schools in the mid-1700s paid their views scant attention, continuing to insist on memorization and the regurgitation of what a teacher had said. Students, like the followers of Confucius, were to find ways to harmoniously integrate into their surroundings and, like the apostles, most were still given the command "Follow me!" Integration and imitation remained important parts of being a student. By the end of the century, though, the views of the philosophers gained some traction. With the popularity of the critical ideas swirling around the Enlightenment, many saw students as those, like Socrates' interlocutors, learning to question the status quo. Students were on a path toward autonomy, leaving behind what Kant called immaturity, the inability to think for oneself because of the forces of politics, religion, or tradition. Education was beginning to aim at more than just economic independence; it strove to cultivate students' ability to make their own judgments, a key ingredient in what it meant to be free. From journalists to professors, from civil servants to teachers, more and more participants in the public sphere argued for this expansive approach to education. Students should, they emphasized, be in the process of enlightenment.

Gradually this link between education and enlightenment began to affect European universities. These had long been bastions of ecclesiastic authority, and students, for all their unruliness, were learning how to fit in and to imitate their teachers. But like so much else in the second half of the 1700s, this too began to change as new areas of inquiry opened, and as the value of an independent mind was elevated in public culture. Now we see developing a new idea of the student, one linked to a new view of the professor. University professors weren't there only to instruct students in more complex matters. They were themselves pursuing open questions and learning while they taught. In Kant's terminology, they were not enlightened; they were, like their students, in the process of enlightenment. This ideal of continual inquiry was being discussed in the professoriate, and it would have an important influence on what came to be called "lifelong learning" in the West.

These notions of independent thought and open inquiry led to a new conception of the university as a place of research, a locus for the creation of knowledge. This would set universities apart from secondary educational institutions and vocational schools, and it would mean that many university students would be expected to participate in the creation of knowledge rather than just passively receiving instruction. This new idea of the university—and of the university student—is powerfully captured in Wilhelm von

—

Humboldt's 1809 treatise "On the Internal and External Organization of the Higher Scientific Institutions in Berlin."[19] Humboldt had been appointed as the minister responsible for educational reform in Prussia, and when he assumed office few had reason to think that the young official would develop a comprehensive vision for the university in its cultural context. But that's what he did, creating an ideal type for an autonomous institution of scholarship and learning that would go on to have an enormous impact on what became the modern research university.[20] The university's ideals would come to have an important influence on how students were understood.

Humboldt himself was tutored at home through high school with a strong emphasis on the classical traditions, and the exposure to ancient Greek culture and civilization left an indelible mark. By the time he was ready for the university, he was swimming in the deep end of the German Enlightenment and encountering the leading philosophical, linguistic, and scientific minds of the day. He attended the university at Göttingen, where Kant's influence remained strong, and did his best to understand the impact of revolution that swept through France in the summer of 1789. Wilhelm entered the civil service in Prussia, and after a stint as an ambassador, public service presented an opportunity to define a distinctly Germanic response to the aggressive expansion of French culture.[21] Napoleon had centralized the higher education sector in France and, with the establishment of the *grandes écoles,* created tight connections between the national government and post-secondary learning. In France, at least in theory, there would be a division between the research and the teaching corps, though both would be in the service of the nation.

By contrast, Humboldt wanted the modern Prussian university to be a place where teaching and research were intertwined, and he thought the state was ultimately best served if these activities took place without its interference. His views are commonly linked to what would be called "academic freedom" in the twentieth century: the ability to pursue research unfettered by either political or commercial interests. "Since these institutions can thus achieve their purpose only if each one, as much as possible, faces the pure idea of science," he wrote, "solitariness and freedom are the predominant principles in their circle." The pursuit of scientific knowledge — be it in religion, biology, or history — meant endless systematic inquiry and open publication and discussion. This pursuit was what differentiated universities from secondary schools: "It is a peculiarity of the higher scientific institutions that they always treat science as a problem that has still not been fully resolved and therefore remain constantly engaged in research, whereas the school deals with and teaches only finished and agreed-upon bits of knowledge. The relationship between teacher and students will therefore become quite different from what it was before. The former does not exist for the latter, both exist for science."[22]

This idea of science, *Wissenschaft*, was capacious, encompassing all disciplines that engaged in rational inquiry and public argumentation. The pursuit of knowledge demands freedom — not just freedom from censorship but also the freedom to organize research in ways that seem to scholars most appropriate to their object of study. According to this idea of the university, students learn to appreciate knowledge for its own sake rather than the immediate satisfactions of vocational instruction. Otherwise, those looking for the practical fruits will kill the very tree that produces those fruits in the first place. The tree of knowledge — science itself — must be allowed to grow in its own way. "The crucial challenge," Humboldt wrote, "is upholding the principle whereby science is seen as something that must be pursued endlessly." One can hear the echoes of Kant's conceptualization of enlightenment as an ongoing process and not a final state. For Humboldt, science and enlightenment were one.

Two Humboldtian concepts are key to understanding what students sought in attending institutions in which teaching and research were increasingly linked. The first is the freedom to study what one wants. In the French system, a centralized curriculum for the entire nation was established for all students. Humboldt envisioned an educational institution in which students could pursue inquiry as they saw fit. It should be said that he also thought certain branches of study (languages and linguistics, for instance) were critical for humanistic inquiry. Still, consonant with the independence he thought crucial for professors, he believed that freedom of inquiry could stimulate the university student to find new paths through a variety of disciplines: "The move from the school to the university is a period in the youth of life, into which the school, if it is successful, places the pupil so purely that he can be physically, morally, and intellectually left to freedom and independence, and, freed from coercion, will not pass into idleness or practical life, but will bear within himself a yearning to lift himself to science, which hitherto had been shown to him merely from afar."[23] It's harder to think for yourself, Humboldt believed, when you are told what you must study. If the drive to learn is linked to freedom, then advances in inquiry can occur.

The second key concept in understanding the student experience at the evolving Humboldtian university is *Bildung*. As this idea emerged in the German Enlightenment, Bildung came to stand for an education that was much more than memorization, more even than training in any trade. Bildung was the formation of the student as a complete person, someone whose various faculties were developed in

---

a complex unity. The point, once again, was not to achieve some final goal, some enlightened state. The objective was to engage in a self-determining process that energized the inquirer and opened new avenues for discovery. In Humbolt's opinion, education links "the self to the world to achieve the most general, most animated, and most unrestrained interplay."[24] This should happen in seminars but also in casual interactions among students. It was important to create the conditions for the free exchange of ideas and experiences because in an atmosphere without compulsion there would naturally arise opportunities for unexpected personal and communal development.[25] In an atmosphere of freedom "saturated with learning," students would be on a path to the self-determination that Kant wrote about in "What Is Enlightenment?" They would be ready to graduate, or to become teachers themselves, when learning had become integrated into their daily lives rather than being something merely scheduled for them by professors. Clearly, learning by yourself didn't indicate your education was complete. It just meant you were more freely determining your own continuing formation.

Humboldt wasn't just a theorist of the university or of education. As an official with thoroughgoing responsibility for restructuring the Prussian educational system, he took concrete steps to implement momentous reforms, putting in motion an integrated approach to learning from elementary school through the university. Each subject area and each period in a student's educational itinerary made sense as part of a coherent whole. His creation of the University of Berlin (now called Humboldt University) was the icing on the cake. Humboldt's ideal vision of the university as an institution devoted to the "inner precision, harmony, and beauty" of scientific inquiry was a lofty one.[26] What was it like to be a student at an actual Prussian university?

Americans who studied at German universities in Humboldt's day reported back on the social life they found there. For all the modernity of the educational ideals, the student culture was decidedly old-fashioned. The American academic George Ticknor, who studied in Göttingen in the early 1800s, was struck by how students formed associations with traditional regional affiliations and rules of honor that entailed frequent dueling. The "system" of student life, he reported, was self-governing, and students were determined to enforce the rules they created. Although sometimes capricious or even violent, this system "introduces into their behavior to one another . . . a degree of order and decorum, and a gentlemanly spirit, which nothing else can give to a thousand young men brought together where they have no responsibility."[27] Ticknor also reported on his work with devoted mentors and his attendance at three lectures a day, "as much as my health will bear." He also notes that he studies for an additional nine hours a week, and he seems proud to be putting in what he thinks of as a strenuous effort. Students in Germany had much more freedom to choose their subjects of study than did their American counterparts. German professors were likewise able to teach topics from their research rather than being bound to repeat a particular series of lectures on a canon of texts. The young American was impressed by this academic freedom and anticipated that Americans would be much more devoted to their studies if they were at greater liberty to choose what they studied. Ticknor was also struck by the separation in Germany of universities from practical and political life. Universities were in their own world, which tended to make their faculties overly theoretical. "A man of science lives entirely isolated from the world; and the very republic of letters" in

German-speaking Europe "has no connection with the many little governments through which it is scattered."[28] Most students entered this isolated world, of course, only temporarily, and they were determined to make the most of the freedom accorded them there. But this wasn't just an individual freedom to study; students set up their own fraternal subcultures of masculine ritual and celebration for as long as they were there.

Decades after Ticknor was at Göttingen, the philologist and professor of languages James Morgan Hart published a report on student life and his own education in Prussia. Hart grew up in New Jersey and spent his undergraduate years at Princeton University before leaving for Europe in the 1860s for further study. He focused on ordinary student life rather than on the star teachers and pupils. "Had my career in Göttingen been an extraordinary one, full of exciting episodes, I should have hesitated to make it public," he wrote. "But precisely because it was so uneventful, so like the lives of my associates, I have deemed it fit to serve as a model for illustration, not imitation."[29] In fact, Hart did have an argument to make about improving American higher education, and it would emerge in his comparisons of the American system with its German counterpart.

Hart noted that students beginning their freshman year in German-speaking universities were a few years older than their American counterparts and, more important, they arrived with preparation in languages, mathematics, and the sciences that was dramatically superior to what was offered at even the best schools in the United States.[30] But it wasn't the case that the first-year students at Göttingen arrived intent on becoming scholars. Like Ticknor, Hart was struck by the student culture – especially the clubs, dueling, and drinking rituals. Small groups of students repaired most nights to taverns, where "the atmosphere was dim and heavy with smoke; groups of students stood around, puffing, drinking, boisterously talking. One or two were practicing 'cuts' [fencing moves] in the corners of the room, to the imminent peril of the ears and noses of any who might stray into their vicinity." Hart was fascinated by the masculine camaraderie and casual violence, particularly because they seemed so at odds with the often-expressed lofty university ideals of Bildung and scientific research.

No strangers to ritualized violence themselves, Americans in the nineteenth century were fascinated by German dueling. The practice had once been common enough in America, but by the 1850s its popularity had begun to wane. The oddity for Hart was to find university students, would-be scholars, so enamored of the practice that they went to some lengths to seek out occasions to use a sword to defend their honor. "It is a notorious fact that nine tenths of the duels are fought without any real provocation; one student happens to bump against the other in the street, or one chaffs the other a trifle too sharply. The students have a code of honor of their own, namely, a list of expressions which one cannot himself use without rendering himself liable to a challenge and which one must always resent." The first-year students were especially prone to being tempted into a duel, and Hart pokes fun at their meager fencing skills and curious costumes. "Bloodshed aside," he writes, "the general appearance of the duelists is very comical. The pad and cravat and spectacles make them look somewhat like a pair of submarine divers in their armor." He is surprised to find dozens of students "going about with bandaged cheeks and noses." In the end, he concludes that dueling among students is an "abominable bit of nonsense" — but, after all, "better than street fighting."[31]

Although drinking, fraternities, and dueling catch his attention, Hart is particularly concerned with the freedom given the

---

German students in contrast to the tutelage, as Kant might have said, bestowed upon American undergraduates. In Germany, once students finish their gymnasium (high school) preparation, they are considered "ripe" for the freedom of study at the core of the Humboldtian university. There they can choose to attend lectures and seminars, or not to attend them. Intellectual work is no longer geared to success on an exam. They don't study together in cohorts or classes, as do their American counterparts. They are, in other words, treated like adults who can make their own decisions. "It will be impossible to understand the character of the German Student without making this element of moral freedom and direct personal responsibility the starting point in our investigations. In no other way shall we be able to account for such extremes of lawlessness on the one hand, such models of industry on the other. Both idleness and industry display an intensity, so to speak, that we shall look for in vain in an American college." Undergraduates in America lack this intensity, says Hart, because they are treated like children: "During the entire period of four years, the collegian is made to feel that he is looked upon as one incapable of judging and acting for himself. His college life is a mere continuation of his school life." The American college delays the students' autonomy by directing their studies and attempting to control their social lives. To recall a phrase from Kant's "Enlightenment" essay, American colleges make it so convenient to stay immature! When you move from high school to college, even if you are traveling away from home, you are still under the supervision of someone who takes parental responsibility for your well-being and, perhaps more important, tells you what to study and whom to study under. "Whereas the German student is the direct opposite. When the young Primaner receives the gymnasium's certificate of 'ripeness' for the university, he knows that his school-boy days are over, that he has done forever with lessons, marks, grades, surveillance, courses of instruction. He is a young man free to select his studies, his professors, his rooms, his hours of work, to regulate the entire course of his life, to be what his own energy and talents may make him."[32]

The freedom given the student means that professors don't oversee the education of undergraduates as much as join them in inquiry, in what Humboldt thought of as the pursuit of knowledge, of Wissenschaft. It was crucial for him that no "external coercion" was applied.[33] If undergraduates choose to waste their time, not attending classes and such, that is their business. Hart notes that many a first-year student does just this, and then comes around to his responsibilities to participate in, assume responsibility for, his own education. "His previous dissipation," Hart sagely observes, "has served to sharpen his wits and give his character a firmer set." Relations between professor and student are not, Hart notes, especially friendly, but they are pleasant enough. Students in the United States are treated like children, and so professors are often put in the position of exercising parental discipline. "The chief drawback to the lot of a professor in America," he emphasizes, "police duty and discipline, does not exist in Germany." Professors at a true research university are not required to "fritter away their valuable time deciding whether Smith was really suffering from the measles or only shamming."[34]

It is not just the freedom to teach and study that the American visitor finds attractive, it is also the equality: "University life has certainly this one merit: it puts all its members on a footing of perfect equality. Distinctions of rank vanish on the Mensur [dueling ground] and in the lecture room. The university court . . . knows no respect of persons. The son of the humblest barber or shop-keeper will get nothing less than justice, the son of the count or baron, nothing more." Students are bound together, at the best moments, "by individuality of thought and freedom of action." Hart is drawn to the sense of accountability this promotes among undergraduates, an accountability that extends to the pursuit of knowledge: "What he studies, he studies with the devotion of a poet and the trained skill of a scientist." This combination, Hart laments, does not exist in the American system because of the tendency to infantilize students in ways that make them intellectually subservient and socially rambunctious. The German student, above all, learns to think for himself—"made to feel every day for upwards of three years of his life that he must weigh all things and judge for himself."[35] To again recall a theme from Kant's essay, freedom does not mean students are enlightened, but it does mean they are in the process of enlightenment. They are, one should be reminded, men. One day they will be joined at the university by women, but that day will not come until the turn of the century.

Hart's reflections on his time at Göttingen were clearly meant to push American educators toward accepting what would become the American research university. In America, however, many professors opposed giving students too much latitude in either choosing their subjects or determining how they would spend their time. Higher education in the United States had always been concerned with "character development" which, apart from traditional Christian moralism, also meant steering the student away from private concerns and toward the needs of the community. Small wonder Rollin's views resonated so strongly in the colonies and the early colleges! America's oldest colleges were affiliated with churches, and they kept a watchful eye over the sinful inclinations they expected to be part of student life. The freedom that so impressed Hart had to be integrated with the character development so important in American approaches to higher education. Could one say merely that whatever character emerges from the free development of the faculties would be good? Not if you thought that there was always a sinful dimension to these faculties. In the United States, when colleges claimed to know what good character was, they seemed to feel an obligation to lead their students toward that goal, constraining their freedom in the process. From old dress codes to contemporary speech codes, these have been controversial.

Certainly, Hart's ideas about freedom and education befitted the Enlightenment orientation of American thinkers like Thomas Jefferson. The founder of the University of Virginia and second president of the United States emphasized that education should "enable every man to judge for himself what will secure or endanger his freedom."[36] The political and moral core of education involved cultivating the capacity for independent judgment in students so that they could properly resist external coercion. Mr. Jefferson's university, as it came to be called, would be an engine of inquiry where the habits of study and reflection, research and conversation, led to the betterment of students and teachers alike. "Education generates habits of application, of order, and the love of virtue; and controls, by the force of habit, any innate obliquities in our moral organization."[37] Part of that moral organization was the practice of freedom while one studied, and in this regard the University of Virginia was more like Humboldtian institutions than its peers in America. In Charlottesville, the plan was to allow students "uncontrolled choice" in what lectures they chose to attend so that they could alter the course of their studies as they learned more about themselves and the world.

Certainly when students thought about freedom, they thought about more than just the choice of classes. In the United States, undergraduates strongly resisted efforts to control their behavior. At

Mr. Jefferson's university, professors who displeased them were subject to ridicule or physical abuse; and the "drunken insubordination" of students was a disconcerting problem for those in charge of the stately campus. American administrators and professors, unlike their German counterparts, thought they had a duty to police the nonacademic lives of their charges. Visiting Germany, the sons of U.S. aristocrats encountered young members of the middle classes, while in the 1800s, most American students were from wealthy families. They were not about to be bossed around by mere schoolmasters. At the University of Virginia, armed students periodically took over the campus. These undergraduates were not interested in their freedom to choose classes but in their freedom to carry weapons, to drink, and to form secret societies. Hart described students at Göttingen entering the adult world of freedom of inquiry; at many American campuses, students wanted the freedom to do as they wished without adult interference.

Rebellious students may have been enjoying the conveniences of immaturity (to use the Kantian phrase), but they were just postponing the day when they would become accountable members of society. This postponement worried Ralph Waldo Emerson because he thought that what students were actually learning was conformity. Puerile undergraduate rebellions presaged adulthoods that would be marked by a desperate urge to fit in with others. It was all too easy to reject the authority of the faculty and think oneself a rebel when, in fact, one was just conforming to one's peer group.

Emerson was interested in how we take in the world and how our intuitions, in collaboration with the world, generate new ways of thinking and feeling. He conceives of the mind not as a passive slate upon which the world leaves impressions but as an active partner with the world. Education, then, will not just be the absorption of knowledge gathered from inquiry and experiments; it will involve an increased awareness, even cultivation, of the self. The point of a student's education will not just be the accumulation of knowledge or even the building of character. The point will be the transformation of the self. Where Humboldt's idea of Bildung concerned the layered formation of an individual in society, Emerson imagined a richer engagement with the world – even if that engagement transformed one's self. The research university reconfigured the relations of teacher and student, Humboldt argued, because both would serve science. This meant that both would work within a discipline for the development of knowledge. Emerson had something else in mind: "We teach boys to be such men as we are. We do not teach them to aspire to be all they can." Emerson pleads with us not to create mere followers by teaching a student to join a school, subscribe to a new dogmatism. This would be to have "foreclosed his freedom, tied his hands, locked [him] up and given the key to another to keep."[38]

Following the dictates of a discipline or a school of philosophy was too limiting for Emerson, foreclosing aspects of experience to which he wanted students to remain open. "Higher education should ignite students' spirit and intelligence with the materials from nature and the past," he wrote, "not merely show them how to digest these materials." "Colleges," he insisted, "can only highly serve us, when they aim not to drill, but to create; when they gather from far every ray of various genius to their hospitable halls, and, by the concentrated fires, set the hearts of their youth on flame."[39] He didn't think it would be hard for colleges to attract students if they inspired them: "If the colleges were better, if they had the power of imparting valuable thought, creative principles, truths which become powers, thoughts which become talents . . . we should all rush to their gates: instead of contriving inducements to draw students, you would need to set police at the gates to keep order in the in-rushing multitude."[40]

Whereas Kant wanted students to be ready to think like adults and Humboldt added a devotion to scientific research as a way for them to think in productive ways, Emerson wanted students to be open to the world and its inspirations so that they could find themselves and their surroundings anew. Of course, students learn specific things, certain skills, but this is not enough: "We exercise their understandings to the apprehension and comparison of some facts, to a skill in numbers, in words; we aim to make accountants, attorneys, engineers; but not to make able, earnest, great-hearted men. The great object of Education," wrote Emerson, "should be commensurate with the object of life."[41]

Emerson wanted more from students than just the mature embrace of the freedom to study that Hart described at German universities. He considered students open to inspiration from a variety of sources and urged that they remain open to the cultivation of self, always receptive to new stimulation. "The child amidst his baubles, is learning the action of light, motion, gravity, muscular force," he wrote. "In the game of human life, love, fear, justice, appetite, man, and God, interact. These laws refuse to be adequately stated. They will not be written out on paper, or spoken by the tongue. They elude our persevering thought; yet we read them hourly in each other's faces, in each other's actions, in our own remorse." The great student, for Emerson, remains open like the child, continuing to search among others for insight and inspiration. The great student needs teachers, but not as oracles of information or masters of methodology: "Truly speaking, it is not instruction, but provocation, that I can receive from another soul."[42] The good student is provoked away from conformity.

—

Emerson believed that true education teaches one not to integrate into society or follow the crowd or its charismatic leader but to discover one's own way. Notice everything and imitate nothing, he advised. Students should "resist the vulgar prosperity that retrogrades ever to barbarism," refusing to trade their souls in the marketplace.[43] They must not confuse education with being trained to do one thing well so that you can sell that skill to another or fit a part of yourself into someone else's enterprise. Students should learn how to be full human beings, not mere appendages, and this means continually questioning what they are doing. Learning how to walk on your own feet, embracing action, and trying out new ideas — these are the tasks of the self-reliant American student.[44] Young people find themselves in "libraries, believing it their duty to accept the views which Cicero, which Locke, which Bacon have given, forgetful that Cicero, Locke and Bacon were only young men in libraries when they wrote those books."[45] "I unsettle all things," writes Emerson. "No facts are to me sacred; none are profane; I simply experiment, an endless seeker with no Past at my back."[46] Some of this sounds like a version of the Socratic tradition of critique, but the American is more affirmative, less ironic than his Athenian ancestor. He wants his audience not only to realize their own ignorance but also to embrace their appetites for adventurous experience. He imagined active, independent students for an active nation that would declare its independence and maturity by rejecting the tutelage of the Old World of Europe.

Chapter 4

THE STUDENT IN COLLEGE

Growing Up Is Hard to Do

When the American academic James Morgan Hart was reminiscing about his Göttingen student days in the 1860s, Germany had yet to be unified as a nation-state and America was engulfed in its bloody civil war. Just a few decades later, the German Empire boasted the most prestigious universities in the world, and America's best students from both the North and South were longing to spend time learning research methods with a sophisticated Germanic intonation. In 1892 one of the most unusual and talented of those students was the twenty-two-year-old W.E.B. Du Bois. Du Bois would become one of the great advocates of learning as a path to empowerment and freedom, and his experience in various school settings reveals much about the modern ideal of who could be a student and what it would mean to find success in this role.

Although Du Bois described growing up in rural Western Massachusetts as a "boy's paradise," he was often the only black person at any gathering. But it wasn't just his race that made him stand out. Du Bois excelled in school to such an extent that his neighbors took up a collection to allow him to continue his education after high school. The citizens of Great Barrington who created a fund to educate the young man thought he'd feel more at home in a southern city with a larger black population than in New England, and so off he went to Fisk University, a private black school in Nashville. It was only while living in the South that Du Bois came to truly feel the intensity of racist oppression enforced by the threat of violence. Taking jobs off campus to make ends meet while he pursued his degree brought the young northerner face-to-face with the reality of Jim Crow segregation. Although growing up poor and fatherless in the hills of Berkshire County had hardly been easy, teaching children in a windowless schoolhouse in the East Tennessee countryside was a rude awakening. Still, some recollections were rosy: "We read and spelled together, wrote a little, picked flowers, sang, and listened to stories of the world beyond the hill."[1] But that nostalgia was always tempered by the realization that all around Fisk segregation persisted and the threat of racist violence was omnipresent. Du Bois conceived of education as a form of empowerment in this context, and he credited this early teaching experience with whetting his appetite for the professional projects awaiting him.

Fisk, like most black colleges and universities at the time, was coeducational, and its curriculum grew out of a liberal arts tradition. The school had been founded by New England Congregationalists who were, in the words of biographer David Levering Lewis, "committed to and consistently successful in producing African-American versions of New England ladies and gentlemen — Black Puritans or Afro-Saxons, as they were sometimes mockingly called."[2] The young Du Bois was struck by the attention students gave to their attire, and he learned quickly that social class could be signified by dignified fashion. The curriculum, which Du Bois found congenial, ensured that students learned the basics in literature, religion, philosophy, mathematics, and the sciences. Young men and women would acquire the "furniture of the mind" that would enable them to think well and to apply themselves to any number of challenges. Student life on campus was meant to amplify the teaching in the classroom. Social relations should be broadly educative – whether you wrote for the school newspaper or sang in the college choir. But segregation of the races was the framework for the black men and women on campus. In Great Barrington the young Du Bois learned from white teachers and classmates, and he advanced by learning how to navigate in the context they controlled. At Fisk the context was black, and the campus culture could thrive only to the extent that it remained protected from the white world around it.[3] In this regard, Fisk was like other historically black colleges and universities, providing their students with opportunities to thrive that were denied them in the wider culture. Fisk was established just after the Civil War, and many of the other schools for African Americans were begun after the Morrill Act of 1890, which specifically granted land to schools for black students.

At Fisk Du Bois learned to appreciate power and leadership, especially in places of great division. His speech at his commencement had high praise for Otto von Bismarck, the Iron Chancellor who made a modern state out of a faction-ridden people. Just as Bismarck had "uplifted" the German people in the creation of the German Empire, so, declared Du Bois, black leaders would raise up the fortunes of their race through education and creativity, creating cultural if not political unity. A fellow commencement speaker exhorted Du Bois's class of 1888 to "do what comes to you, keeping your eyes open to the world, and in due time God will bring that work to your hands for which you are best fitted." From its mission-

—

ary origins to the ministers' speeches at commencement, religion permeated Fisk, giving students a sense of duty, a feeling of obligation to do the right thing for a people not yet a generation removed from slavery. At that same commencement, the Reverend C. S. Smith reminded students (as did many speakers in the years to come) that their education should prepare them not just for personal success but to make a contribution to those around them. "After reciting the political history of the Negro," the *Fisk Herald* summarized, "[Smith] advised the young men to seek their sphere and try to fill it. Our young men must not only imitate but originate." The encouragement to "originate" is not that far from Kant's call to emerge from self-imposed immaturity, nor from Emerson's emphasis on the creative inspiration stemming from openness to experience. Du Bois himself was the editor in chief of the *Herald,* and like many student journalists he wasn't concerned only with lofty ideals and aspirations. In his final editorial for the paper, the young man waxed sentimental about the end of his time at Fisk. As beloved students graduated, even the mice in Jubilee Hall wept, he wrote. The editor, Du Bois said, would like to "write more at length, he would expiate, but (tears) emotion chokes his utterance. Goodbye gentle grumbler, may your sun ne'er go down," and, ending with a joke, "May you ever be joyous and never edit the HERALD."[4]

After leaving Fisk and before he headed to Germany, Du Bois studied at what was America's premier institution of higher education, Harvard, the college of his "youngest, wildest visions." The Fisk graduate would find, though, that while his Harvard professors were better known than those at Fisk, they were not always better teachers. Du Bois did have the good fortune in Cambridge of studying with giants of philosophy. Harvard had initiated its elective system, giving students real choice in what they would study, and Du

Bois chose to attend the great pragmatist philosopher William James's lectures. James would become his "friend and guide to clear thinking." Excluded from much of campus social life because of his race, Du Bois would excel in his studies, on which he concentrated with real discipline. Through James, he did get invited to the Philosophical Club to hear conversations "at the highest level," and he read Kant in a tutorial with George Santayana. As his biographer Lewis put it, he "was taken seriously . . . because he took the life of the mind so seriously." Du Bois himself would later say he was drawn to "the lovely but sterile land of philosophic speculation." The ambitious young man found real success at Harvard as a writer and orator. He also found racism in his interactions with white students and remained outside their social circles. "I asked nothing of Harvard but the tutelage of teachers and the freedom of the laboratory and library," Du Bois wrote. "I was quite voluntarily and willingly outside its social life."[5]

If he was rejected by the glee club or snubbed by Boston's elite, he didn't let it slow him down. He wrote that he was "in Harvard but not of it," though he would be selected as one of five speakers at the graduation ceremony. His commencement address on the kind of civilization that could produce a Jefferson Davis was widely applauded at the time as a star performance.[6] He completed an additional two years of undergraduate work at Harvard as well as a master's degree. (Later he would return to Harvard for his doctoral diploma.) Continuing on to study in Germany would be another dream come true.

Having achieved academic successes at Harvard, Du Bois set his sights on attending the University of Berlin, and he was determined to land a fellowship that would take him there. He was confident that he could earn it on his intellectual merits, but the color of his skin got in the way. Du Bois discovered the Slater Fund, set up in 1882 to help black students, but the funds were directed toward "industrial education," by which was meant "manly occupations like those of the carpenter, the farmer, and the blacksmith." Most of the funding went to the vocational training championed by Booker T. Washington and the Tuskegee Institute rather than the liberal arts curriculum of institutions like Fisk and Harvard. But some members of the Slater Fund organization were open to a more general education for black men eager to make contributions to their communities. The head of the fund was former U.S. president Rutherford B. Hayes, who put it this way: "If there is any young colored man in the South whom we find to have a talent for art or literature, or any especial aptitude for study, we are willing to give him money from the education funds to send him to Europe or to give him an advanced education, but hitherto their chief and almost only gift has been that of oratory." Du Bois was offended that the former president, who had done so much to put an end to Reconstruction as a path to racial equality, claimed he couldn't find qualified black men for advanced university work aside from oratory. And so the young scholar at Harvard offered himself: "I respectfully ask that I be sent to Europe to pursue my work in the continental universities, leaving the details of the work to the recommendations of the appropriate professors in Harvard."[7]

Hayes responded that he had been misquoted and that the Slater Fund was not looking for a black liberal arts student. Du Bois replied angrily. He accused Hayes of insulting the entire race by implying they should be trained only for plowing or preaching. "I find men willing to help me thro' cheap theological schools, I find men willing to help me use my hands before I have got my brains in working order, I have an abundance of good wishes on hand, but I never found a man willing to help me get a Harvard Ph.D." Du Bois would later relate that Hayes told him to reapply, and that when he received the positive news of his fellowship, he rushed to New York, "walking on air." He also reported buying a $3 shirt ("'bout four times as much as I had ever paid for a shirt in my life") to mark the occasion.[8] As it turns out, Du Bois, not unlike many of his fellow students, used fine clothes to mark his status as a serious person who was going places.[9]

In the summer of 1892, Du Bois departed for Germany. As a black student he expected to be treated very differently from his white compatriots, but he was used to that. The student venturing abroad was beginning to be a recognized type in American letters, and many a young person of means was able to break free of parochial conventions by leaving the United States. Du Bois followed in their footsteps. Already he had left home twice to pursue educational dreams, learning along with his studies more than most about the varieties of American racism. Despite his achievements, those lessons were a consistent reminder to know his place in the world. But Germany would be different. Of course, the Old World had prejudices that ran deep, but they didn't run principally along the black/ white color divide. The voyage there felt to Du Bois like a slow release from the pressure of his own country's ongoing efforts to protect white supremacy. When the ship arrived in Düsseldorf, he joined a family for a tour and was quickly impressed by how little his skin color mattered to his new acquaintances. He adored the medieval town of Eisenach and, says Lewis, "Out of range of his American demons, he seemed to grow lighter, almost playful, and more accessible with each week."[10] Dora, one of the daughters of the family with which he was staying, shocked the young scholar by proposing marriage to him.

Du Bois found his study abroad experience educationally as well as socially liberating; he built on his Harvard experience to find opportunities to study with faculty at the cutting edge of their respective fields. In particular, he steeped himself in the new social science methods emerging from the University of Berlin, methods that would before long be at the core of American sociology. Unfortunately, his doctoral dissertation in German wasn't enough to earn a degree as he hadn't been registered for the required number of semesters. The Slater Fund members probably disapproved of the broad liberal learning that complemented his research project—it wasn't practical enough for their tastes. In any case, the fund wouldn't continue to renew his fellowship, and so Du Bois returned to America to submit his work for a PhD at Harvard instead. On the ship back to the States he wrote in his notebook: "As a student in Germany I built great castles in Spain and lived therein. I dreamed, I loved and wandered and sang and then after two long years, I dropped suddenly back into Nigger hating America."[11]

The freedom of being a student in America at the end of the nineteenth century did include dreaming, loving, wandering, and singing—for white students. Du Bois was both an anomaly and an exemplar—as a black man, his learning and liberty were constantly shackled by the ubiquitous racism in the United States. And yet he worked at the highest level, overcoming the obstacles that were put before him and taking advantage of opportunities as they arose. Studying in Germany allowed Du Bois some respite from the pressures of racist institutions; it allowed him to experience the dignity of being a student with the freedom to explore his own potential in the company of others who were also learning about themselves and the world. The return to the United States was also part of his education, of course, harsh as this was. In this country, his life as a student would always have to fit inside his life as a black man. In a country determined to preserve white supremacy, black men and women had to struggle mightily for the status of student, a status that implicitly recognized one's open-ended human potential.

Of course, Du Bois was hardly a typical student, but the deep research skills he employed in his advanced work built on the traditional liberal education he received as an undergraduate. Industrial school offered a quite different model for student life at black colleges around the turn of the twentieth century. These institutions eschewed liberal learning in favor of training in a trade that young men and women could put to immediate use. Alabama's Tuskegee Institute, founded in 1881, was the paragon of this educational model, and its leader, Booker T. Washington, had achieved great fame by the time Du Bois was an undergraduate at Fisk. Washington preached the gospel of vocational learning as the path to economic independence, and the student experience at places like Tuskegee was dominated by nonacademic work. Students might attend classes two or three days a week, but the rest of their time was spent practicing a trade — be it farming, cabinet making, or building houses. Indeed, many a library at the industrial schools was built from the ground up with student labor. When Washington raised money for black schools, he emphasized that he was not unsettling the status quo in race relations so much as providing young black men and women the opportunity to become economically autonomous rather than upwardly mobile at the expense of whites. His schooling was meant to create financial independence for the students without disturbing the white establishment.

Women students at schools like Tuskegee had a sphere of labor separate from that of men. Margaret Murray Washington was principal there. She had graduated from Fisk, where she had been editor of the school newspaper and head of one of its literary societies (and a friend of Du Bois). It was there that she met Booker T. Washington, her future husband, when he came to deliver a commencement address. He hired her at Tuskegee, where she directed a focused vocational education for women focused on domestic work; she went on to become a national leader in connecting the education of black women with expertise in the "practical arts." The idea was not merely to train women for domestic service but, in the constrained circumstances of the Jim Crow era, to enable them to teach others while also earning income.

Women students at Tuskegee had an additional burden: showing they weren't becoming "too educated" by attending school. Men were afraid of educated women for a variety of reasons. There were some who feared that girls who excelled as students wouldn't be satisfied with the realities of family life, but the Tuskegee principal disagreed: "We firmly believe that this plantation colored woman will prove not 'a menace' to the race, but a deliverer, for through her will come the earnest, faithful service for the highest development of home and family that will result in the solution of the so-called race problem."[12] Home and family were not at all in tension with education, in her view; indeed, schooling would enhance the role of women in the home by giving them the virtues and the skills needed to create middle-class domestic spaces. But most poor blacks worked during the day and could not find time to go to school during the traditional hours. Margaret Murray Washington started a network of women's associations (clubs) whose mission was to create educational opportunities outside of the conventional school day for laborers — men and women. More advanced students at Tuskegee joined alumni in teaching at night in surrounding communities:

"Cooking, sewing, brickmasonry, painting, carpentry, have been the most important subjects taught," wrote the principal. "Many a man and woman, boy and girl, are today in this town and county able to make a decent and comfortable living because they had the chance to attend this night school." Although the emphasis was on helping students to make a living, subjects like Negro history were also part of the curriculum: "We believe that any school which does not teach children to know and revere their own men and women of note, fails in its duty, and the Tuskegee Woman's Club has lent its influence in this direction." Students at Tuskegee were apprentices in living well and living right, and they were expected as alumnae and Club Women to continue to live the motto "Lifting as We Climb."[13] In this context, being a student didn't mean merely learning how to achieve economic independence, or even to realize one's individual potential; it also meant learning to do right by one's community. This was a lesson meant to last a lifetime.

Building character, elevating the virtues through proper socialization, was at the core of student life in institutions like Fisk and Harvard alike. For young women in the late 1800s and the first half of the twentieth century, formal learning beyond high school was still a rarity, and when it existed it often had a strong religious component. Growing up in a small Illinois town, Jane Addams dreamed of going to a sophisticated Northeastern school for college and had her heart set on a newly founded institution for women, Smith College in Massachusetts. Although not religious herself, she had a powerful desire to serve others, and the elite women's college represented to her the possibilities of a broad education that would be a prelude to becoming a physician. She longed for what she saw as the more cosmopolitan world of ideas far from the Midwest. Jane's father recognized her potential, but he also worried about what he took to be her "fragility" and decided to send her closer to home to a less demanding academic environment. Less than one-half of 1 percent of American girls attended college in the 1870s, and even families like the Addamses who prized education hesitated. So, in the summer of her sixteenth year, Jane was sent to the Rockford Seminary for Women. "My father's theory in regard to the education of his daughters implied a school as near home as possible," she would write.[14] Traveling would have to come later.

Rockford was an evangelical institution, though some of the students, like Jane, professed little religious feeling. With less rigorous admissions standards than Smith, the school provided students of varied academic preparation with a community of learning, led by women, that offered resources for intellectual and spiritual development. Jane was disappointed not to be heading to New England, but she made the most of the resources at Rockford. Literary societies, which Jane's biographer Louise Knight describes as "boot camps for citizenship," were vehicles for learning outside the classroom, and in these groups Jane excelled, honing her ideas while sharpening her ambitions. She wrote for the school magazine and became its editor. Supported by teachers and the friendship of her fellow students, Jane argued in her articles for women's rights to independent thought and action. In Knight's judgment, her participation in culture and society served as replacement for religious devotion. Serving others, especially the most vulnerable, became a spiritual practice for many who were attracted to the "social gospel" of American Protestantism. As a student, Addams would learn to experiment with ideas, be comfortable with ambiguity, and to debate. In her senior year, she participated in a statewide oratorical competition in which she was the only woman participant. Although Jane would never get to Smith College, her undergraduate years at Rockford set her on a path of intellectual exploration and social service.[15]

Smith College was founded in 1871 by Sophia Smith, who was determined to provide the "means and facilities of education" equal to those available to men. The campus was designed to ensure that young women were protected and felt at home while they studied. Although bookish Jane Addams dreamed of attending Smith, it's not at all clear she would have met its rigorous admissions standards, which "included basic Greek and algebra through quadratic equations and some geometry." The seminaries and "normal schools" that women attended did not expect this level of preparation, and most featured modern languages rather than Greek and Latin. Smith College, though the first to be endowed by a woman, was modeled on nearby Amherst College. Those drawing up plans for the new college wanted it to be a viable alternative to the all-male schools. These institutions were being pressured to co-educate, and the existence of a strong women's college relieved some of that pressure. Smith also gave women opportunities for social life beyond the hedonistic fraternity boys at nearby Amherst.[16]

Northampton was selected as the site for the women's college, with the intention of connecting the lives of the students with the everyday life of a small but bustling New England town. The college was not to become a convent walled off from the outside world. These students would not be isolated from practical life, and the small cottages in which they lived on campus would resemble family homes rather than the unnatural "hot-house environment" of a large dormitory.[17] The goal was to make the college feel like a traditional home but with modern, professional educators. The plans for the college included no campus library or chapel. The young women would go instead to the local library and churches, much as someone might wander into town from her parents' home. When the first fourteen students matriculated, they were supervised by a "lady-in-charge" and a female faculty member. This system continued even as the college expanded. With this proper supervision and integration into the life of the town, few formal rules were needed. The young ladies could participate in local religious and civic associations. The students would grow into "refined, intelligent, Christian woman-hood."[18]

Providing higher educational opportunities for women remained controversial in early twentieth-century America — even if it was to be in a single-sex environment, which some worried presented its own temptations. For example, the eugenics movement was gathering steam at the beginning of the 1900s, and adherents were convinced that allowing intelligent girls to become students was an offense against nature and a distraction from family life. They should instead be having babies! Places like Smith were said to waste "the best blood of the American stock . . . [sinking] it in a dry desert of sterile intellectuality and paralytic culture."[19] It was true, apparently, that graduates of women's colleges did marry later and did have fewer children than less educated women. Some administrators at women's colleges responded by introducing more "domestic science" into the curriculum, both to make family life more attractive to their students and to placate the critics.

But in the wake of World War I, increasing the lure of domesticity was not top of mind for administrators at women's colleges. Students were calling for more freedom at co-educational schools as well as women's colleges. Undergrads at Smith and other schools wanted less supervision, especially with regard to their socializing with men in town or invited onto campus. Many women's colleges had a "10 o'clock rule" that required a "horizontal position" and lights out at the appointed hour. In the second decade of the twentieth century, women students were demanding to be less sequestered, less regulated, and more self-governing. As men were supposed to be learning to govern themselves – to become autonomous – women, too, agitated on campuses for more freedom. Students at Mount Holyoke, for instance, used the language of the Enlightenment when they demanded "self-imposed discipline" as opposed to "externally imposed discipline."[20] Many of the regulatory flashpoints involved socializing with men. The 1920s was a period in which expressions of heterosexuality were more acceptable in polite society, and whereas campus life at women's colleges once revolved around all-girl plays, literary societies, debating teams, and sports, students now found opportunities to bring men onto campus (or be driven to their campuses).

Leaving behind some of the concerns of previous generations, families of means began to expect their children to attend an institution of higher learning, and increasingly this included the girls. The women's colleges, like other elite schools in the Northeast, were populated by undergrads from prominent families or those that had recently enjoyed professional success. For Jane Addams and her cohort back in the late 1800s, a college education was a rare opportunity to set off on a new course in a wider world of learning and cosmopolitan concerns. By 1900, about 35 percent of those enrolled in post–high school study were women. Young women like Addams had had to fight for the opportunity to continue their education. By the 1920s, as Helen Horowitz notes, "going to college was the thing to do," and almost half of those doing it were women.[21]

Of course, here we are speaking of young "ladies" of privilege, many of whom were used to having people answer to their needs.

Once at a women's college, they were learning to excel without the pressures of a patriarchal world in which freedoms for women off-campus were hard to come by. Their early success in intellectual work and careers raised alarm bells in the establishment, and men tried to "feminize" women's education, by which they meant make it more conducive to producing helpmeets than professors. At the same time, though, women students — well aware in the aftermath of suffrage of how women could overcome traditional constraints — were demanding the right to smoke, to study and socialize when they chose to do so, and to have men on campus at their invitation. College authorities pushed back, much as they did at colleges where the students demanding more freedom were men.

Pushing back is what higher-education administrators learn to do. College authorities have long had an adversarial relationship with undergraduates. If we circle back to colonial times in the United States, we find that the small numbers of young people at college found the rules of faculty and administrators overly restrictive. On the cusp of adulthood, they resented being treated as children. In the wake of the American Revolution, students complained of the dictatorial tendencies of faculty and presidents, linking them with the recently overthrown British.[22] We saw in the previous chapter that during the early days of the Republic, Jefferson tried to provide students at the new University of Virginia with more intellectual autonomy. The students there rioted for more *personal* autonomy; coming from entitled families, they didn't take well to the rules of campus life. They were used to seeing their own families make the rules — or to get what they wanted when they wanted it. This was the case at many colleges in the nineteenth century. Students exerted pressure on schools to meet their "needs," to live up to a young person's notion of what it meant to *live like a college student*. As historian of education Frederick Rudolph has noted, "Unquestionably the most creative and imaginative force in the shaping of the American college and university has been the students."[23] The shaping didn't usually have to do with the content of classes or even the contours of the curriculum. Those students at the University of Virginia in the early 1800s wanted to socialize and carry weapons without so many rules, while students at Princeton caused an uproar to protect their fellow classmates from being too harshly punished for disobeying the faculty and its code of academic conduct. These were not undergraduates belting out a Kantian "Dare to know!" They just wanted to ride horses through the campus in the middle of the night, carouse, and fight; and they made a show of their independence through insolence. The "standard tricks" played on instructors included locking them in their rooms, dousing them with water, and ensuring that they would trip and fall while moving about the campus.[24] The perpetrators of these pranks were a new class of human beings—no longer children but not quite adults. They were "college men" defending what they perceived to be a certain way of life. The pious American hope to use higher education to instill morals and character development in the students seemed to call forth its opposite: young people determined to create a lifestyle defined by their own enthusiasms.

Throughout the nineteenth century and the first half of the twentieth, that way of life was available to only a very small percentage of the male population and an even smaller percentage of females. By the turn of the twentieth century, though, the percentage of young people enrolling in instruction after high school started to grow, reaching almost half the population by the 1970s. Today it is

—

even higher, with more women than men earning degrees. Initially, the college way of life was hypermasculine, with students making a show of male bonding, violence, and physicality. But as large public universities became increasingly co-educational in the later 1800s, male rituals took a beating. As historian of education Michael Hevel notes, "Coeducation continued to be controversial in large part because of women's success at college, with 53% of Bachelor of Arts degrees awarded to women in 1899 at the University of Michigan."[25] It is reasonable to think that some of the reasons male college rituals became more anti-intellectual, even anti-educational, had to do with the academic success of women on campus. Why compete in a contest you are unlikely to win?

But before we get to those rituals, which express both a desire for autonomy and a desire to be unaccountable, we might consider again why educators thought that students living and learning together was such a powerful combination. Recall that Rousseau argued that other people were a negative influence on learning because they stimulated vanity and the desire to imitate. Although the residential college has roots in England, it is a quintessentially American creation. Literary historian Andrew Delbanco underscores how the notion of the campus is related to the ideal of the living Church in colonial New England — unity emerging from the multiplicity of voices in the congregation. The "disparate gifts" that people bring to the Church are what contribute to its vitality, its ability to be "a light unto the nations." Similarly, he writes, colleges have emphasized the educational virtues of diversity: "College was about young people from scattered origins converging to live together — taking their meals together, attending lectures and sermons together, sharing in the daily rhythms of study and social life. At the heart of this "collegiate way" was a concept of what might be called lateral learning — the proposition that students have something important to learn from one another."[26] This ideal has developed in various shapes and sizes over the last two hundred years or so, but it has consistently animated a vision of what students bring to a community of learning. Students are not there merely to receive instruction; they are there to participate in and contribute to education as a communal journey.

One can see the conflict between the spiritual ideal of a community of learning and the rough-and-tumble reality of conflicts between faculty and students. While undergraduates fought to protect the college way of life from the academic toil required by classes, open battles tended not to go so well for the young men. Presidents and professors had the power to expel individual students and even to suspend classes if things got too unruly. So resistant strains of student culture flowed underground, finding ways to lubricate a way of life outside the classroom while displaying just enough obedience inside academic spaces to stay enrolled. This is the culture of *the college man* who saw himself "at war" with the institution's authorities and with any students who collaborated with them: "Nineteenth-century college professors had a clear notion of the good student. They tried to form him through penalties and rewards. Faculty offered students high grades, membership in honor societies, and awards for excellence. Those who called themselves college men created an alternative system that distributed status by their own standards, not those of professors, and denigrated the good student."[27] A real college man didn't seek his professor's approval but instead competed with other young men in drinking, card playing, and sports. A nineteenth-century memoir of American college life stressed that there was general "approval for all means calculated to circumvent those in authority — provided that these means are employed for the benefit of those who make no pretensions as scholars."[28] The standards of success used by college men in the early twentieth century had to do with getting ahead in an increasingly corporate America, something that the faculty seemed to know little about. The college student was "a careless boy-man," someone "who shirks his work and deceives his instructors in every possible way."[29] This was a different model of the student from what we've seen thus far. The goal was not to arrive at independence and maturity—it was to delay such an arrival for as long as possible while showing a capacity to be a manly team player.[30]

Fraternities became the vehicle of choice for protecting this oppositional student culture. They created their own subcultures and hierarchies, and they enforced their own rules through hazing and a variety of physical and social punishments. Many schools tried to ban secret societies, but in the end most settled for co-opting them. Unable to enforce their institutional rules in the fraternity houses, their basic strategy was simply to implore them to make their own "rules" less discriminatory, less violent, and less dangerous. Since fraternities were born from the revolt against institutional authority, this strategy never had more than limited success.

Especially in their early years, fraternities replicated the patterns of elitism and discrimination found in American society more generally. Most fraternities wouldn't accept Jews or blacks, and Catholics didn't have an easy time, either.[31] People of modest means also had a hard time getting in. Those looking to college as a path to upward social mobility would not find it within most fraternities; that kind of overt ambition was beneath the college man. Students seeking to improve their prospects would try instead to succeed in the official academic dimensions of the university. But the fraternities, and the sports teams associated with them, promised post-college success, too. Athletics turned out to be a powerfully useful

—
127

way to allow students to compete outside the classroom while also stimulating loyalty to the institution. Those who strove successfully for leadership positions in fraternities or were successful athletes were told that these achievements were the *real* predictors of social and economic success, not the artificial academic world. The "school of football" was frequently discussed by well-placed alumni who touted the survival of the fittest as a way of justifying the violence among college men. By "survival" these folks meant success, usually in the business world. "Soft skills" – or now "power skills" – of teamwork, leadership, and resilience were what one really learned as a college man – and one learned these outside of and even in spite of classes. "What constituted dominant masculinity changed over time," Michael Hevel notes, "with debating skills in the antebellum period replaced by drinking skills in the twentieth century."[32] It's not hard to see the link between the violence of fraternity subcultures and the effort to ensure that one's manhood would never be questioned.[33]

In the early twentieth century, most college women were at co-educational institutions, and as fraternities grew in power there, women students found ways to organize their own social lives. Sororities were born to create social hierarchies parallel to those that fraternities set for men, though at first the women's organizations were more defensive than rebellious. Some sororities had more status than others, providing women students with a guide to what was most socially respectable – even those who found themselves at the bottom of the pecking order seemed to agree about which sororities were at the top. With changing sexual mores in the middle of the 1900s, sororities took on the additional function of policing romantic relationships. Once the codes of fraternal masculinity changed so as to make college girls desirable targets of their attention, sororities had a new source of prestige – arousing and controlling sexuality.[34] Women students tended to be more socially conservative than their male counterparts, and sorority sisters more conservative still.

There were important demographic changes at colleges in the 1930s and 1940s. An influx of immigrants put pressure on the traditional collegiate culture. The newcomers were more than willing to compete, but with the growth of larger corporations and of the professions, being a good sport and a member of the right sorority or fraternity no longer ensured financial success after graduation. Specific skills and "smarts" were increasingly sought after by employers, and in the hiring process they began to look for evidence of academic achievement. For those looking to move up in the world rather than protecting the status their families had achieved in previous generations, academic success became essential. As the professional class grew, and as the schools that trained its members became more selective in the wake of World War II, grades became more important for post-college success. You might want the collegiate way of life, but if you were planning on going to law school, say, you'd better earn decent grades.

Many of those looking to move up in the world saw a college education as the pathway to improved economic status. After World War I there was some financial aid available to veterans or to survivors of soldiers killed in the conflict, and after World War II this was dramatically increased in the United States with federal legislation that provided educational benefits for those who served in the armed forces. There is some question about how great an impact the legislation had on steering people who would not otherwise have gone to college, but there is no doubt that the presence of veterans on campus powerfully affected the image of college and its culture. Even elite institutions *seemed* more democratic with regular GI Joes now attending classes. These men didn't feel the same need to prove their masculinity in fraternity rituals. Unlike the younger men aspiring to be "big man on campus," the veterans were busy using their college educations to launch their postwar lives.[35]

On many campuses in the Northeast, veterans put pressure on fraternities to end their discriminatory practices. These students were older and had had more contact with people from beyond their family's social circles than traditional undergraduates. Some expressed their chagrin that they had fought against bigotry in the war only to find it entrenched in their colleges and universities. Many schools had quotas for Jews, and few made a place for black students. Within a year after the end of the war, for example, returning soldiers at Wesleyan University were urging campus leaders to dismantle the discriminatory practices that had long been taken for granted. And many small colleges did exactly that, although in some instances this meant that a local Greek organization had to sever its ties with the national fraternity.[36]

How about those who didn't pursue social advancement through Greek organizations, those who didn't strive for prestige among the popular kids? There were, of course, many students who did not aspire to run social clubs or think that war with the faculty was the point of campus life. The members of elite Greek organizations might have looked down on them, but how did those focused on college learning think of themselves as students? In the nineteenth century, many of them would have seemed destined for the ministry — not a bad path for bookish young men with little financial backing. In the twentieth century, economically disadvantaged students saw their studies as a pathway to the professions. Whether it was because of social ostracism, economic disadvantage, or pure intellectual curiosity, these were undergrads who discovered a world of ideas on campus. Some aimed at academic prizes and honors, fulfilling the hopes of their teachers and earning their recommendations for graduate or professional school. For others extracurricular activities like reporting for the school newspaper provided their more valuable learning experiences. Fraternity culture itself could be the target of exposés, as were the spending practices of profligate university administrators. College reporters were sharpening their writing skills and their political views. Some discovered ideas on campus that led them to angry debates mirroring those taking place in the wider world. This was fairly common at the City University of New York, for example, where warring radicals hashed out their ideological disputes in the lunchroom rather than in a political philosophy class. As Irving Howe remembered, he felt little interest in academic disputes of the professoriate. "I'd go to class, sit impatiently for a few minutes until the roll was called, slip out, head for the lunchroom where a political argument was waiting, and at the hour's end race back to get the books I had left in the classroom."[37] It was in the lunchroom that Howe thought he was learning to think for himself, to leave behind "self-imposed immaturity," by listening to and debating with others.

By the 1950s, some on campuses were debating about the most effective ways to stem the tide of corporatization, while others were networking as best they could to join a professional elite that would lead them to lives in fancy suburbs. Fraternities and sororities remained strong, and in the postwar period administrators learned how to co-opt their rebellions into collegiate loyalty. Alumni looked back fondly on the institutions that had allowed for Greek life, and school spirit was closely identified at many institutions with athletics. But there were other experiments going on, as college men and women explored cultures, ideas, and emotional attachments different from the ones they had known in their families. At Wesleyan University in the 1950s, for example, avant-garde music and art percolated among teachers and students alike. A small liberal arts college in central Connecticut with Methodist roots, Wesleyan became the center of conversation among radical thinkers like inventor Buckminster Fuller, composer John Cage, intellectual historian Carl Schorske, mystical classicist Norman O. Brown, and Marxist philosopher Herbert Marcuse. It was in the 1950s that innovative interdisciplinary curricular ideas were hatched and the arts broke away from their narrow focus on Western classics. Anthropologist David P. McAllester and musicologist Richard Winslow joined in the effort to envision creativity and culture in ways that were less beholden to conventional Western ideas of individualism and private property. By the 1960s their experiments would dramatically alter college life and spill over to affect the broader culture.

Although the percentage of female college students fell from the Great Depression to the immediate postwar years, the sheer number of women students was always growing. Opportunities for women graduates were not growing, however, and it's not all that surprising that many dropped out before finishing their degrees. Although women were successful students, they did not receive as much help from their schools as men did in developing careers. In *The Feminine Mystique* (1963) Betty Friedan excoriated the society that left her fellow Smith College alumnae disappointed in their lives as housewives, and she powerfully called into question why America was failing its talented women. In the post World War II period, even affluent white women who graduated from schools like

Smith were finding career pathways obstructed by male prejudice. Academic opportunities were blocked by the favoritism of the old boy network, and professional advancement was often foreclosed by male executives who thought a woman's place was in the home. No wonder that after a couple years of college many women often saw marriage as a strategic move that seemed safer than taking one's chances applying for jobs or graduate school.[38]

African American women faced the most career obstacles. At many colleges, the graduation rates of black women were low, but still as a group they found ways to leverage their educational experience as they moved into positions of leadership in churches, clubs, and other civic organizations. Their student years may seem to have been less about Enlightenment notions of overcoming immaturity than about empowerment through skill development and acquiring the confidence to participate in a highly segregated public sphere. Yet in another sense black women were using various strategies to break their enforced dependence. Black Greek organizations played an important role in this regard. Like their white counterparts, black sororities and fraternities signaled social status on campus, but they also incubated a culture of talent development and community service at odds with Jim Crow America. At Howard University, the Alpha Kappa Alpha (AKA) sorority "disciplined" students to conform to an image of respectability. Hairstyles, clothes, decorum (from what one ate to whom one dated) were all regimented and enforced by a culture that included hazing and social ostracization. But this sorority also helped its members understand the wealth of "culture, pride and activism" that came with serving the wider black community beyond the borders of the university.[39] Since it was founded in 1908, AKA has inspired service and civic engagement — from protests against lynching to literacy campaigns in the early part of the 1900s, and from supporting greater access to health care to fighting for desegregation even before the explosion of activism in the 1960s. Today the sorority has over a thousand chapters and three hundred thousand members.

With some notable exceptions such as the women in AKA, students at residential colleges in the early to mid twentieth century tended to focus their political energies on parochial campus concerns. Students might want more freedom *while they were enrolled*, but they were largely unconcerned with national or international issues. Perhaps it was inevitable that this would change as a much broader swath of the population found its way to large public universities or small leafy colleges. As campus populations came to more closely reflect the population of the country, national issues entered higher education. In the early 1960s, national struggles for civil rights seized the imagination of thousands of students around the country. Many traveled to the South for voter-registration drives or participated in boycotts of businesses that refused to integrate their premises. When these young men and women returned to their schools, they had experienced another form of education. They were politically motivated to become agents in the public sphere, not just recipients of instruction or singers in the glee club.

The country was changing, but the young people entering college in the early 1960s wanted it to change faster. At a time of intense civil rights battles and the acceleration of the war in Vietnam, the pleasures of campus social life seemed trivial to increasing numbers of vocal students, and the promised rewards for good student behavior seemed empty. When the University of California at Berkeley tried to tighten restrictions on campus political activity, students created the Free Speech Movement not just to defend their right to express themselves but to challenge the framework of society that offered what its most famous leader, Mario Savio, called a sick "utopia of sterilized automated contentment." He went on to underscore that "an important minority of men and women coming to the front today . . . would rather die than be standardized, replaceable, and irrelevant." This was early in the decade, and Savio's inspiring rhetoric wasn't aimed only at changing the campus; it was directed at an entire society that made use of students as "raw material" to be pushed into an economic machine that would shape them into efficient units. We are not just the material of an educational institution, he said, "we are human beings!" He wasn't just claiming the right to *say* these things. Savio was urging his fellow students to stop the evils produced by the system through civil disobedience. His words became an inspiration to young people around the world: "There's a time when the operation of the machine becomes so odious, makes you so sick at heart that you can't take part! You can't even passively take part! And you've got to put your bodies upon the gears and upon the wheels, upon the levers, upon all the apparatus — and you've got to make it stop! And you've got to indicate to the people who run it, to the people who own it — that unless you're free the machine will be prevented from working at all!!"[40]

Savio's was an inspiring version of the student not only as an autonomous individual but also as a free member of a community. He and his compatriots saw "immaturity" being imposed on students by those in charge of the university, and he underscored that the students rallying around the country wanted to really learn, not merely be trained to become cogs in the industrial order. They weren't just occupying the administrative building, keeping the university from conducting business as usual. They intended to hold their own kind of classes there, to imagine a more humane education. "We'll do something which hasn't occurred at this University in a good long time! We're going to have real classes up there! They're gonna be freedom schools conducted up there! We're going to have classes on [the] 1st and 14th amendments!! We're gonna spend our time learning about the things this University is afraid that we know! We're going to learn about freedom up there, and we're going to learn by doing!!" In 1964, Berkeley students demanded a more authentic learning experience, an education in freedom.[41]

American students from coast to coast were echoing many of the values underscored by the *Port Huron Statement,* issued in Michigan by the Students for a Democratic Society (SDS). The SDS articulated broad goals of social and economic change, and their manifesto depicted students as agents of transformation. Many of us, it said, "began maturing in complacency," but events in the world and the political conscience of young people were provoking calls for radical change. "We ourselves are imbued with urgency, yet the message of our society is that there is no viable alternative to the present." The university itself fosters complacency when it should be empowering students to think for themselves and imagine alternatives to the status quo. "Tragically, the university could serve as a significant source of social criticism and an initiator of new modes and molders of attitudes. But the actual intellectual effect of the college experience is hardly distinguishable from that of any other communications channel — say, a television set — passing on the stock truths of the day." The SDS statement called for transforming universities from mechanisms for reproducing the hierarchies of society reigning at the time into catalysts for critique that would open new avenues of real change. As "the only mainstream institution that is open to participation by individuals of nearly any viewpoint," universities were particularly well positioned to create "communities of controversy" to awaken various social groups both to the injustices around them and to the possibilities for radical change. Students had the potential to be at the vanguard of a new historical moment, and they had the potential for creating alliances with other social groups eager to create a different kind of world.[42]

Student activists in the 1960s had come a long way from Kant's genteel rhetoric of slowly pursuing maturity through a gradual process of enlightenment. They were even further from the Confucian students who very consciously learned to situate themselves in relation to previous generations in an effort to create harmony over time, or from the student as disciple following the call of a teacher who embodied the word of God. Many students throughout the West in the 1960s saw themselves as a vanguard of critique, and it may be tempting for that reason to see them in the Socratic tradition of unmasking elites whose knowledge is built on shaky foundations. But Socrates taught an ironic skepticism, not rebellion based on new certainties about how one should live. The radicals agitating for change in the 1960s went beyond the siren songs of skepticism toward a passionate embrace of the music of politics in a new key.

In the years following the *Port Huron Statement* and Savio's famous speeches, more and more students made demands for freedom on campus and beyond—the kinds of freedoms they hoped would transform how society was structured. When they protested oppressive hierarchies and restrictions at school, they also had their eyes on the hierarchies and restrictions that were dominant in the society of which the university was a part. Sometimes they began with something very specific—say, changing academic requirements—and at other times they demanded a meaningful role in the most strategic elements of school governance – from hiring and promotion to decisions about the allocation of financial resources. And it wasn't just the always visible groups of outsiders and radicals who were opposing the status quo. By the late 1960s, even some fraternity and sorority members came out to protest. The civil rights movement motivated many, as demonstrations against segregated America moved from the South to cities and towns across the country. The war in Vietnam was even more decisive in igniting opposition to "the establishment." Enrolling as a student might protect young men from being inducted into the military for a time, but the risks of dying for a cause few understood or believed in were real. If one lost one's student status, one could be conscripted into the military and sent to Southeast Asia. Universities were asked to provide the authorities with lists of students at risk of failing out because of their low grades. The government's oppressive tactics weren't abstract; they were very tangible. Between 1967 and 1969, the number of students who opposed the war doubled to almost 70 percent. For many young people in college, the Vietnam War destroyed complacency about following governmental authority. Young people were being sent to fight a war they didn't believe in, a war that many judged to be downright evil.[43]

Meanwhile, as the struggle for voting rights and desegregation morphed into the Black Power movement on many campuses, African American activists pressed for institutional change on their historically white campuses. This could take the form of calls for special housing arrangements for black students, for more affirmative action in admissions, or for the addition of black studies to the curriculum. In New York City's universities these changes created many more opportunities for African American and Puerto Rican undergraduates and faculty.[44] At San Francisco State College, students built a coalition of what we would now call "students of color" and conducted a strike demanding curricular and admissions reform. African Americans, Asian Americans, Chicanos, Latinos, and Native Americans came together to demand equity, and for some this became a model for future activism.

Although at any particular school only a minority of students might have been out protesting, by the end of the decade, students had declared themselves on strike at more than 350 colleges in the United States. This protest movement was part of an international rejection of the status quo. In 1968 street protests erupted in Berlin, London, and Paris (among many other cities) to reject government officials and conventional political parties. "All power to the imagination!" read the radical graffiti in the Quartier Latin. Students in the streets were creating a festival of alternative ways of living. By contrast, the brutal failures of the war in Southeast Asia symbolized the callous, if not criminal, rigidity of a capitalist society that had once promised an openness to innovation and creativity. Kant's hope that through education one would gradually learn to think for oneself without disturbing current hierarchies seemed at best naïve to students who clamored for different modes of *feeling* and a total liberation of the mind. As it turned out, many student protestors were themselves naïve about the willingness of the forces of order to put down demonstrations they deemed truly threatening. Around the world, protest groups were routinely infiltrated by law enforcement, and leaders were targeted. In the United States, the killing of unarmed student demonstrators at Jackson State and Kent State in 1970 was a tragic reminder that the forces of order, too, could "bring the war back home."[45] The police and national guard were often willing to use violence to defend the hierarchies in which they had found a place. Richard Nixon's decisive re-election in 1972

139

made clear just how far apart the world of activist students was from that of their fellow citizens. Older generations struggled to understand why so many of those fortunate enough to be enrolled in higher education now turned their back on a culture that gave its young people so many opportunities. The young were incredulous that the older generations failed to heed the calls for change.

Within a few years, though, student culture itself seemed to mutate in ways quite different from what the radical idealists had hoped for in the late 1960s. Although the "protesting student" was one of the identities young people could adopt on campus, by the middle of the 1970s, it was no longer the dominant note in the chords played at most colleges and universities. With the end of the draft and the war in Vietnam, the economy was once again calling the tune as many students saw higher education as an opportunity to audition for jobs and social advancement.

Chapter 5

THINKING FOR ONESELF BY LEARNING FROM OTHERS

Public consciousness at the end of the 1960s was preoccupied with student life and youth culture. Although undergraduates were always just a minority of young people, their protests, sex, and music drew the scrutiny of worried pundits, parents, and politicians. Very few people seemed focused on the curriculum when there were protests to attend (or complain about) and new forms of community to imagine (or critique). However, within a few years of the killings of students at Kent State and Mississippi State, and as the threat of being drafted for the war in Vietnam subsided, a shift in campus culture took place. Students were no longer so preoccupied with politics, communal purpose, and changing the world. Unruly protestors gave way to careerists interested in getting good grades and positive recommendations to professional schools. In the mid-1970s one could certainly still find campus radicals, but the energy had shifted to libraries, science labs, and the kinds of experiments in ways of living that could be conducted in the privacy of one's own dorm.[1]

For all the dismay and bewilderment expressed by the older generations about student culture in the 1960s, enrollments were

141

surging. The boomers wanted their children to have access to higher education, and colleges during that decade attracted more young people than ever before. The number of American college students more than doubled between 1960 and 1975.[2] These young people also attracted the attention of commentators from presidents and vice presidents to local op-ed writers, all expressing chagrin at where those students were headed. Campuses had become screens upon which the broader culture expressed its anxieties about political and social change, economic dislocation, and the decline of traditional mores. Critics on both the left and the right weren't questioning the modern Enlightenment idea of learning as a journey for overcoming self-imposed immaturity so much as doubting whether the new crop of students were on that path. Whether accusing students of radicalism or conformism, apathy or grade grubbing, nearly all critics bemoaned the inability of undergraduates to think for themselves.

The question of when exactly students *are* supposed to think for themselves doesn't have a clear answer. Learning can be focused on skill acquisition rather than (or as a prelude to) the creative development of autonomy. It may even be the case that before one can become a student capable of throwing off immaturity, before one learns freedom, one must acquire a certain competence through imitation and repetition. Athletes and musicians know this well, and they spend countless hours repeating drills and scales. At what point do they become performers in their own right? How does one graduate from drills to become capable of autonomous learning? How does one learn to become a learner and not just a trainee? After all, training doesn't necessarily lead to autonomy; many kinds of living things can be shaped without those things developing agency. You can "teach" a vine to grow up a trellis, and trees learn on their own to adapt to their soil and their atmospheric conditions. And sometimes one may think one is training another only to find that from a broader perspective one is really part of a different pattern. For example, armed with enough treats, I can teach my dog to sit, wait, and then come when I call. And now when we go for a long walk, I find she lags behind, waiting for me to give some "commands" so that she can then come and get her treat. Who is training whom? Should we talk of autonomy in this situation, or is it more like entanglement?[3]

Pets and domestic animals, like children, depend on us for their basic needs. But we don't expect nonhuman animals to graduate to independence, even if they do clearly get us to do their bidding from time to time. Human students of any age increase their capacity for independence as they become adept at language use. To use a language well is to use it creatively, to speak for oneself and not just repeat someone else's words. One of the most important paths in this regard is facility with written language. As we acquire the ability to read on our own and to express ourselves in writing, we enormously expand our possibilities for gaining access to information, and for autonomous judgment. But how should we pass this ability on to children? Do we treat them as smaller versions of autonomous thinkers, or more like pets to be trained?

In order to address these issues, it's helpful to step back a bit in our chronology. The questions of how to teach people the language skills that would lead to autonomy were not just theoretical in the second half of the nineteenth century, especially in the United States. As the right to vote was expanded, and as a formal education became more economically useful, employers and elected officials expressed increasing interest in improving literacy rates. With increasing numbers of voters and more complex jobs, the country and its economy needed more readers. But how best to accomplish this? Should learning to read exemplify the freedom of thought and creativity that advanced students prized, or should it resemble a disciplined army drill team that learns precision moves through intensive practice? In the 1880s, humanistic education reformer Horace Mann argued that students shouldn't be bored to death with repetitive exercises in sounding out letters. This, he was sure, left them in a position of subservience to the instructor and did nothing to foster a love of reading. Instead, he argued, they should be treated as whole persons who could derive meaning from letters grouped into whole words. Letters were only "skeleton-shaped ghosts," Mann wrote, and he wanted students to learn to think — and not just memorize — as they learned to read.[4] In the early twentieth century, psychologist G. Stanley Hall, philosopher John Dewey, and others picked up on what they called the "whole word" method of teaching reading, thinking it would be appropriate for students who were becoming creative, autonomous citizens in a democracy. This was, it seemed, the enlightened view of the student as a person who should not be narrowly educated, whose creativity should be fostered through holistic learning. Progressive education adopted teaching the whole person, and so it seemed only natural that reading was to be learned by stimulating a desire to understand the meaning of whole words.

Unfortunately, this approach to building literacy just doesn't work as well as repetitive drills to sound out letters, which came to be known as phonics. Since the mid-twentieth century, decades of research have made clear that the only really effective way to teach children to read well is to build up their abilities to connect letters with sounds and then to amplify those connections through repetitive practice — phonics. Developing skillful behavioral patterns through drills amplifies the neurological networks that undergird language. Students of language must imitate before they can be autonomous; they must be trained before they can be enlightened. Across the world and across languages, children have to acquire the same neurological foundation in order to be skilled readers. They must become "alphabetic," and this requires instruction, feedback, and practice. New computational models have helped us understand the iterative process through which new readers suddenly start recognizing patterns linking graphemes to phonemes. Children may be haltingly sounding out words, but when instruction is successful, young brains are growing more capable of recognizing patterns connecting marks on the page to sounds and sounds to meaning. "Readers build neural structures that represent these statistical patterns and tune them every time a text is read," neuroscientist Mark Seidenberg tells us. Children don't need to memorize explicit rules, but they do need to accumulate "sufficient linguistic and experiential data to bootstrap the meanings of more and more words once they occur."[5]

Ever since the 1920s, when so-called progressive educators displaced the phonics researchers, angry debates have ensued between those who want to build skills through drills and those loyal to a more "holistic" conception of reading. The latter was said to be more "ethical" because it was compatible with the image of a student as someone practicing autonomy while reading for meaning, not just repeating sounds. Researchers like Seidenberg and commentators like American linguist John McWhorter rail against teacher-education programs that emphasize wholeness and meaning at the expense of basic literacy skills.[6] You can't experience freedom and autonomy as a reader without these skills. It is now clear that phonics is an essential ingredient in bringing students to a level at which they can read on their own, but some education programs are so wedded to the image of the autonomous student that they resist learning through drills. *This image of the student is getting in the way of learning to read,* a skill that, once mastered, will eventually lead to the ability to think and communicate more independently.

Although research shows that phonics drills are decisive in helping children learn to read, we have also come to understand that drills and memorization are not enough for achieving another key goal of early education: basic math skills. Many young children learn simple addition and later multiplication through memorization. If the teacher asks, "What is 6×7" and you answer, "37," the response might be "No, it's 42." Students are supposed to glean from this that it is important to *remember* the times table so that next time they can give the correct answer. But a skilled teacher of math wants the student to be not just a better memorizer but also a better reasoner. This requires the teacher to become, as education writer Elizabeth Green calls it, a "mind reader," trying to think through the reasons why students make the particular mistakes they do. "It's one thing to know that 307 minus 168 equals 139; it is another thing to be able to understand why a third grader might think that 261 is the right answer," Green tells us. "Mathematicians need to understand a problem only for themselves; math teachers need both to know the math and to know how 30 different minds might understand (or misunderstand) it. Then they need to take each mind from not getting it to mastery."[7] Once the "logic" of the mistake is understood, the teacher can help the student find a better way of reasoning. This goes beyond memorization to forms of reasoning that the student will use to continue to learn. And that's the key to great teaching at any level: cultivating in students the enhanced capacity to think for themselves in productive ways when they are no longer in the classroom. This is so much more than following a rule or showing discipline, although both rules and discipline are likewise critical parts of the learning process. Helping a student move to mastery in arithmetic requires understanding how that person is already reasoning. Helping a student move to mastery in reading depends on practicing the connections among sounds, letters, and meaning. Repetition helps build a foundation for expansive language use. In all cases, with a solid foundation, mastery means being able to apply what works in one case to other cases — and to do so on one's own. It means becoming students who think for themselves with the tools and the practices acquired from others. That's the basis for thinking freely.

Schoolteachers throughout the twentieth century hoped to transition their students from establishing basic foundations through drills to cultivating independent thinking through creative practices and experimentation.[8] For some this meant, as it did for the followers of Confucius, thinking in such a way that one could find one's place harmoniously in one's society. For others, it meant acquiring enough independence of thought to freely choose to follow an authentic leader. Across the United States, there was hope that education and Christianity could move forward together — that education would further inspire the followers of Jesus to character development and good works. There were also many teachers in the Socratic tradition for whom independent thinking meant a skepticism about received knowledge. For them, progress was built on recognizing that our received ideas could be replaced by sounder concepts and values. By the time students graduated from high school, they should have the ability to recognize how they might fit in, whom they might follow, and which traditions in their society were ripe for critique. These critical abilities would make graduates more effective citizens.

College students were notoriously suspicious of convention and received wisdom in the 1960s, but many professors by the 1970s found their undergraduates disappointingly immature — unprepared for independent thinking. Their students wanted only to know how to repeat the right answers, get good grades, and advance on well-trodden paths. "By 1976," historian Helen Horowitz notes, "students thought it more important to acquire 'training and skills for an occupation' and get a 'detailed grasp of a special field' than to get along with people or formulate life goals, their strongest preferences in 1969."[9] The mid-1970s were a time of diminished economic expectations, and undergraduates felt pressure to continue their education as a hedge against these bleaker prospects. Just a few years earlier, some students were staying in school to avoid the draft. Now it was downward social mobility that was frightening; now there was more intense competition for the high marks that would lead to admission to prestigious professional schools that, in turn, would provide protection in a risky economic environment. Undergraduates, it seemed to many, were becoming increasingly apolitical as they retreated to the private sphere to nurse their economic anxieties. The lifestyle changes ushered in by the 1960s (sex, drugs, and rock and roll) persisted through the 1970s, but they were just more symptoms of a retreat from the political. The music one liked was a recreational choice, like the substances or the sex one preferred. It was not a protest against or for anything else. Allan Bloom led a chorus of critics in saying campuses were losing sight of the core values of a liberal education in favor of vocationalism while simultaneously cultivating conformity through a consumer-oriented hedonism. He famously sounded the alarm that universi-

—

ties had "appeased" the students' political demands in the 1960s, "offering them every concession other than education." Meanwhile, he claimed, the "longing" that undergraduates used to bring to their studies was dissipated in crude campus pleasures. In words that have aroused conservatives for decades, Bloom judged that "the various liberations wasted that marvelous energy and tension, leaving the students' souls exhausted and flaccid, capable of calculating, but not of passionate insight."[10]

Bloom's criticisms of listless universities and students were not calls to return to Kant's Enlightenment notion of leaving behind self-imposed immaturity. Kant was imagining the gradual emancipation of citizens from their automatic obedience to authority. Bloom imagined a time when the brightest minds would gravitate not toward autonomy but toward a respectful, guided inquiry into the enduring questions pondered by great thinkers of the Western tradition. Although he seemed unaware of any traditions outside the West, we might notice that he took a Confucian integrative approach to education.[11] He lamented that the best students at the most selective universities were not deeply engaged with canonical philosophers. Such an engagement mattered more than anything else one might learn, he thought, since it was through wrestling with the tradition that one developed into a fully human being, someone who had the chance of living a truly human life. For Bloom, the best students wanted to understand their nature, and education was the path of fulfilling or perfecting that nature. But an inquiry into how to live a truly human life, he argued, had become an almost impossible challenge in the modern American university. "As it now stands," he wrote, "students have powerful images of what a perfect body is and pursue it incessantly. But deprived of literary guidance, they no longer have any image of a perfect soul, and hence do not long to have one. They do not even imagine that there is such a thing." Bloom had strong political and aesthetic differences with post-1960s generations of students, teachers, and administrators, but it was the university's abdication of its responsibility to imagine genuine perfection or greatness that particularly provoked his ire. "It is precisely the routinization of the passions of the Sixties that is the core of what is going on now," he wrote.[12] Under the guise of tolerance and democracy, students were being molded into creatures who could no longer respond to the most important and enduring questions. Those, unsurprisingly, were the questions that Bloom had been taught to value when he himself was a student at the University of Chicago.

Bloom's critique of higher education was first published in the *National Review* in 1982, and a few years later his proposal for a book based on it was purchased by an editor at Simon and Schuster. The original title was "Souls without Longing," but the marketing department made adjustments in hopes of increasing what they feared would be very modest sales. *The Closing of the American Mind* appeared early in 1987 and by late spring it was selling like hotcakes. It became a beach read and was at first highly praised even by those in the higher-education establishment that it attacked. As literature professor Louis Menand said at the time, "It gratifies our wish to think ill of our culture (a wish that is a permanent feature of modernity) without thinking ill of ourselves."[13] By turning his magazine article criticizing young people into a best seller for the cranky older generation, Bloom established a model to which op-ed writers frequently aspired. But his surprise best seller was not just a cri de coeur from someone whose favorite texts were no longer attracting the attention he'd been taught to give them. It was also a diagnosis of the flip side of tolerance: nihilism and the inability to take ideas or character seriously. When everyone has a right to their opinions and all opinions are to be treated with equal respect, there's no reason to develop a meaningful perspective on the good life, or to seek Truth. Higher education in the 1960s and afterward was telling students to live "their own truth." For Bloom, following his teacher Leo Strauss, this was a problem endemic to modernity, accentuated in consumer-oriented capitalism. In the contemporary world, the only thing that mattered was the judgment of the market, and so there was no point in exploring important or enduring questions concerning the essence of justice, the perfection of the soul, or the compatibility of politics, religion, and philosophy. The market dictated where one should direct one's attention; the crowd taught us how to participate in trends, and the result was a race to the bottom. Bloom's conservative fans tended to ignore the economic dimension of his critique, enamored as they were with the particular spleen with which he wrote about the 1960s. Rather than blame contemporary university culture for the market economy's destruction of the foundation of Western culture, they excoriated higher education for fueling the energies of civil rights, feminism, anti-imperialism, and sexual liberation—the things that had offended them about youth culture from the Free Speech Movement to Woodstock. Bloom's book continued to have strong sales into the 1990s, and by then it had inspired a chorus of critics, some who attacked the book and others who joined in the book's critique of higher education. Conservative critic and editor Roger Kimball has enjoyed his loathing of college culture as much as any of member of the Bloom fan club: "The Age of Aquarius did not end when the last electric guitar was unplugged at Woodstock," he wrote. "It lives on in our values and habits, in our tastes, pleasures, and aspirations. It lives on especially in our educational and cultural institutions, and in the degraded pop culture that permeates our lives like a corrosive fog."[14]

Presumably, the pop culture fog was especially corrosive for the unformed and directionless student. Conservatives blamed the universities. Giving a pass to the market and relativism – Bloom's targets – they aimed at a more sinister enemy: teachers who indoctrinate the young with their own political views. Bloom didn't believe that faculty or students had particularly strong views about anything, but for conservatives in the 1990s and in the first decades of our century, the great problem was "tenured radicals" corrupting the young. Rather than being relativists, Kimball wrote, they "tend to be indefatigable proselytizers, bent on winning converts in their war against the traditional moral and intellectual values of liberal-arts education."[15] The problem wasn't just multiculturalism as a form of disengagement from philosophical truths, it was Marxist, anti-Western university teachers convincing students to abandon the very traditions on which the universities were founded. In the 1980s, the liberal historian Helen Horowitz had bemoaned the transformation of student life away from political engagement toward the pursuit of economic success.[16] Conservatives writing in the 1990s and early 2000s complained that teaching, scholarship, and learning (at least in the humanities and the interpretive social sciences) had become political indoctrination. These critics believed that the problems had begun when the great works of the Western tradition were replaced in the curriculum by lesser contemporary works favored by multiculturalists: "When students begin reading Frantz Fanon instead of John Locke in their political philosophy classes, something has gone terribly wrong," Kimball complained.[17] The complaint isn't specifically about Fanon or any other author. The notion is that there are some works that have stood the test of time in the West, and that it behooves us to understand these works if we are to understand ourselves.

Nobody seemed concerned with the "test of time" when it came to the sciences and the quantitative social sciences — they were supposed to be working on contemporary issues. No one expected the physics department to be teaching students pre-Newtonian ideas, and the biologists were meant to be introducing students to the latest experimental findings. But worries about "presentism" in the humanities took off in the 1980s along with concerns that professors weren't teaching the same texts or using the same approaches that were in vogue in, say, the 1930s. Fears about losing the tradition often dovetailed with anxieties about race and gender. Given changing demographics in higher education, it's not surprising that teachers added to the curriculum works produced by women and nonwhites. Conservatives saw these additions as disrespectful to the great works of the past, and they believed that the identity, or "positionality," of the authors of canonical works in a core curriculum was irrelevant to their merit. These debates rage on today.

The battles over the curriculum show us how fraught the idea of students developing the maturity to think for themselves had become. Professors believed they were teaching "critical thinking" skills in the Socratic tradition, but commentators accused them of saying, "Follow me!" to their vulnerable potential disciples. Confucian harmony was nowhere to be found. Whereas Bloom blamed students for caring more about their bodies than their souls, conservative critics over the next twenty years tended to blame the faculty for corrupting the youth through their ideologically driven choices about what and how to read. Some commentators thought that student taste (like American taste in general) had degenerated, but most complained that it was the professors who were not setting

—

their sights high enough when they strayed from the canon to teach courses focused on popular culture or contemporary issues. In mocking the salacious titles of papers given at Modern Language Association meetings or syllabi listing books unrecognizable to older alumni, critics were not exactly exonerating students. But they were making them victims. When students did act politically, that, too, was blamed on the faculty. Both undergraduate protest and narrow-minded pre-professionalism was laid at the door of pampered, radical professors manipulating their passive (unfree) pupils.[18]

Without guidance from professors oriented toward the traditional humanities, undergraduates grinding away for the grades to get into a top-tier graduate program or to secure a top-notch internship showed little interest in enduring questions addressed by essential books of Western culture. In the past, wrestling with those books had helped students grow into maturity and avoid following their teachers or the latest fashion among their peers. In recent years, young people – and the culture from which they emerged – have been subject to a different sort of critique, one that aimed at the relentless will-to-achieve that drove students, especially at elite colleges and universities. It wasn't just that students were ambitious, it was the narrowing of their ambitions to achieve something measurable – they were driven primarily by dreams of making money. In a 2014 magazine article and a popular book the following year, culture critic and former literature professor William Deresiewicz memorably labeled these strivers "excellent sheep." Under the guise of intense academic work, he argued, undergraduates were learning how to conform. Like Allan Bloom before him, Deresiewicz worried about the herd mentality on campus. But whereas Bloom thought the problem was a lax moral relativism masquerading as a commitment to equality, Deresiewicz believed that the neoliberal creed of market success was driving the herd. The smart kids wanted the good internships and the good internships were in consulting and finance. They were good because they led to jobs that paid very, very well. In the winner-take-all economy, you either went for the gold ring or you were a loser.[19] Thinking for oneself, being on an enlightenment path to maturity, might get in the way of learning how to fit into the privileged slots that the economic regime offered to students it considered the brightest. We've seen that since the eighteenth century being a student was increasingly linked to thinking freely, but today the idea of freedom has been increasingly displaced by the lure of economic advantage. By the end of the twentieth century, especially in the United States, a good school was one that put students in positions to seize those advantages.

For many Americans today, being "a good student" in high school means competing against other young people for admission to a college that will lead to a successful career. Even though most high school graduates never contemplate applying to colleges with competitive admissions, extraordinary amounts of public attention are bestowed on the hundred or so colleges and universities that accept fewer than half their applicants. This perpetuates the idea that the "good students" are those winning spots at colleges and universities that are difficult to get into. Many institutions are invested in the belief that those who are accepted are more worthy than those who don't make the cut. Somehow the belief is sustained despite an admissions process that is opaque to outsiders and despite clear evidence that the more elite the school, the more likely it is to preserve existing hierarchies of wealth and prestige. Today, upward mobility is harder to come by via education in the United States than in many other industrialized countries, and perhaps it's for that reason that young people here seem so committed to meritocratic competition. Whether they

—

actually prepare people for effective leadership or not, elite schools reproduce economic and cultural elites. The legitimacy of these existing hierarchies depends on commitment to the meritocracy.

The interconnections among students, competition, and economic privilege have all been forged fairly recently, and it's important to remember that more than 80 percent of American students in higher education attend colleges that accept more than half of applicants. Fewer than fifty schools today accept less than 20 percent of their applicants; for rejecting so many, they receive an extraordinary amount of publicity, publicity that ends up further increasing demand and reinforcing their exclusivity. The focus on exclusive schools distorts our picture of what it means to be a college student. In the 1970s, the situation was very different. Stanford, for instance, which today is near the top of the selectivity race by admitting about 5 percent of those who apply, accepted a third of its applicants in the 1970s. At the end of the 1980s, Johns Hopkins University still accepted a majority of those who applied, and in the 1990s the University of Chicago admitted more than three-quarters of applicants. Today both schools' acceptance rates are less than 10 percent. These decreasing acceptance rates have been made possible in part by marketing campaigns aimed at improving an institution's magazine ranking. For the last thirty years, elite schools have worked to become ever more exclusive as if this were indicative of the quality of the education they offer. The best students go to the best schools. How does one know which students are the best? They are at the schools that are hardest to get into – those that reject the highest percentage of those who want to attend. Or so the logic goes.[20]

Belief in the quality of elite schools depends on confidence in the fairness of how they select students. For seventy-five years, leaders in higher education have worked in fits and starts to create admissions processes that would at least appear legitimate. From standardized tests to generous financial aid to affirmative action, colleges have developed criteria for admission that would allow successful applicants to have faith in the process – to not assume it was rigged in favor of the privileged. They've questioned, for instance, the role that family connections and wealth play in the selection process. The goal hasn't quite been to achieve legitimacy through equality; there has been no attempt to make all schools equal or to treat all students the same. The latter could be achieved through some form of admissions lottery, but then those who were accepted at elite schools would just feel lucky rather than chosen or gifted. The elite schools try to legitimate their exclusivity by promoting the idea that they are curating a campus community to maximize the educational outcomes for all who are part of it. In choosing who will be students at their institutions, elite schools also promote the notion that their approach to student selection enhances upward mobility. If they could be seen as launching good students regardless of background into successful careers, this would be evidence of enhancing equality of opportunity. The colleges would be linked to a broader culture and economy that were fair and thus legitimate. Not everyone gets the same outcome, but opportunity is evenhandedly distributed, and schools use methods such as affirmative action to compensate for long-term injustices. Selective higher-education institutions had only to promise to admit students fairly, to sort through applications and find those people with the potential to make the most of their education. Taking into account contextual factors like race and socioeconomic conditions were meant to be important aspects of a fair process. Colleges and universities in this way promoted upward mobility without picking the ultimate winners.

———

Alas, things have not worked out this way. The sorting process of admissions to elite schools tends to find students who already have every advantage, students whose preparation for success is built on inherited privilege. The most selective schools are famously filled with the children of the rich. At dozens of such institutions, there are more children from the top 1 percent of the income scale than from the bottom 60 percent. College leaders often point to the injustices of K-12 education as a way of explaining this imbalance. Wealthy families and the communities of which they are a part are able to provide better primary and secondary education. Their children are not just privileged, they are well prepared. This is not news. Indeed, the standardized tests developed after World War II were meant to cut through the advantages of elite high school preparation. The creators of these tests hoped to better identify natural student potential. But money helps prepare people for these tests, too, and so standardized testing has reproduced the inequities it was meant to address.

The modern idea of the student as someone on the path to freedom, to thinking for oneself, is undermined by these criticisms of higher education. The charges of unfair admissions, like the criticism of political groupthink or mindless grinding away to get grades and internships, attack the integrity of learning as a path to freely thinking for oneself. If the opportunity to study is unevenly made available to people, then it should be rejected by a thoughtful person who recognizes that the education offered is really corruption. If going to college means participating in one's own indoctrination, then one could find no enlightenment there. But even if the critics are right in significant ways about the failures of higher education, many people are still finding in colleges and universities opportunities to explore the world and themselves in ways that are difficult to find anywhere else. If one wants to explore cultural forms that have fallen out of favor, as did Confucius and his followers, a college campus usually offers resources to do exactly that. If one wants, like Socrates and his interlocutors, to challenge existing hierarchies by exposing the ignorance of others, a university can be a place to develop one's skills. Jesus promised his disciples a spiritual rebirth, and today one can find many undergraduates who feel transformed by their education. The critics of higher education want it to live up to the ideal of being an opportunity for learning freedom. So do its defenders. Despite all its shortcomings, so do many of its students.

Learning freedom will mean very different things to students depending on what they bring to their education. Learning opportunities may seem like lifelines to people who have suffered from the inequities of an economic system that produces greater inequality and that fails to protect the most vulnerable — but these opportunities can also feel like traps. Although attending an elite institution can be transformative for low-income students, it can also be an intensely alienating experience. Professor of education (and former low-income student) Anthony Abraham Jack has detailed the myriad ways that a college environment can fail to address the well-being of students who depend on institutional support for many of their basic needs. When a university closes its dining hall for spring break, for example, some of its low-income students go hungry or have to depend on soup kitchens. When most of the jobs available to students on financial aid require them to serve or clean up after wealthy students, class divisions are reinforced. Students who have insecure housing or are supporting family at home can be marginalized in campus cultures that have developed over the years with other constituencies in mind. "Elite universities are now a bundle of confusing contradictions," Jack emphasizes. "They bend over backwards to admit disadvantaged students into their hallowed halls, but then, once the students are there, they maintain policies that not only remind those students of their disadvantage, but even serve to highlight it."[21]

In the last decade, students and administrators have worked cooperatively to address the challenges faced by low-income students in higher education. Rather than being subject to shame and stigmatization, undergraduates facing these challenges have come together to form communities of mutual support. A decade ago at Wesleyan, a student leader whose experience of deep poverty growing up was fundamental to his identity approached me about creating an official residence for low-income students who were the first in their families to attend college. At the time, he was less interested in hearing about the promise of upward mobility than in connecting with other people who had experiences like his own. The idea of rising above his low-income status was appealing, but it also felt like a betrayal, a source of shame. On campuses sensitive to questions around identity, this ambivalence resonated. In the early 2000s, the designation "first-gen student" or "FGLI student" ("first-generation low-income student") was born.[22] The 1998 amendment to the Higher Education Act of 1965 singled out students whose parents had not received baccalaureate degrees as being deserving of special support.[23] The rationale is straightforward, even if the definition of who counts as a "first-gen" student is murky: "Students who were the first in their families to go to college were in general less likely to apply to and enroll in college after controlling for student performance, family income, school characteristics, and parental involvement in their education."[24] Programs for first-gen-low-income students now abound at colleges and universities across the country, and there is an FGLI Consortium that serves administrators at more than one hundred selective institutions. Many admissions offices at selective schools track their percentages of first-gen students and are eager to improve on this metric. Just as a student could be a "rebel" or a "nerd" — recognizable subtypes on campus — a student today can be "FGLI." Since neither of my parents went to college, students and colleagues often ask me what it was like to be a first-gen student in the 1970s. I explain to them that there were no first-gen students then because that identity category hadn't been created yet. Until a group identity is created in a culture, you can't belong to that group. Today, the emergence of first-gen and FGLI means, at least, that more students can face the challenge of being in college as members of a community with a shared identity. For them, learning freedom will mean something different than it means for a wealthy, well-connected student.

Still, despite the pride expressed by FGLI students on campuses around the nation, very few college students hope *to remain* in the low-income brackets after graduation. Indeed, opportunities *are* created for students from modest circumstances who wind up at selective colleges. Just under 20 percent of Harvard undergrads are eligible for Pell Grants, and they certainly do receive a mobility boost from their connection to the school. More than half of them will end up in the top economic quintile after graduation, while the chances for that kind of mobility in the United States is otherwise under 2 percent. And this is not the case just for Ivy League institutions. Selective colleges that support student success on campus also promote upward mobility after graduation.[25] The young man at Wesleyan who requested identity-based housing for low-income students went on to work for a major technology firm and encourages his peers to "pay it forward."

———

Learning how to advance economically is hardly the same thing as learning freedom, whether we have in mind low-income students supporting their families or wealthy students just trying to earn more than their peers in a contest for privilege. Success stories of graduates from selective colleges in the United States highlight how much these universities are part of the culture of meritocracy, despite the fitful rebelliousness of some of their students. The best college students are defined as the ones who *make it* through the tightest filters. Thus, educational institutions are absorbed into (and in some ways come to define) the contemporary regime of meritocracy. "Selective colleges and universities became irresistibly attractive," as philosopher Michael Sandel notes, "because they stood at the apex of the emerging hierarchy of merit." This is a hierarchy that allows people who have economic success and social status to believe that they have earned their place and that the process that has placed them at the top is just. In this hierarchy of merit, being a student has less to do with coming into one's maturity as a thinking and judging person and more to do with being sorted into one's proper place in a competitive economy and society. From this perspective, the system of higher education is a sorting machine in which those who rise to the top are increasingly distanced from everyone else. Employers offering high-paying jobs turn to particular institutions for hiring not because they believe students there learn so much but, as Sandel underscores, "because employers have faith in the sorting function these colleges perform and value the meritocratic honor they bestow."[26]

The student, in this meritocratic universe, is always competing with others to find out who the real winners are. Learning is recast as a competition that will allow for the best to emerge in whatever field is being studied. This has nothing to do with the way learning was conceived by Confucius, Socrates, or Jesus. There were certainly rivalries, but their students were learning in ways that were not strictly competitive. Today, students are taught to constantly evaluate where they stand in relation to their peers. As you will recall, that's why Rousseau thought it was so important that Emile not be around other students: he would be too concerned about how *they* were doing and how *they* regarded him to ever learn about his own capacities. How far we are from those concerns! Today, as young people prepare themselves for the winner-take-all economy, they are primed to do whatever it takes as students to end up with a prestigious job and *not fall behind*. Falling behind has become the contemporary equivalent of sin. One is supposed to desire what others desire so that one can compete with them more effectively. Those who don't get the first prize often strive with even more intensity to ensure that they won't fall too far down the meritocratic ladder. "Even as inequality has widened to vast proportions, the public culture has reinforced the notion that we are responsible for our fate and deserve what we get," Sandel laments. "It is almost as if globalization's winners needed to persuade themselves, and everyone else, that those perched on top and those at the bottom have landed where they belong."[27]

Students play a key role in the meritocratic system because they occupy a supposedly liminal space where the hierarchy is still being established. But the quest for a legitimate sorting process that would justify the vast inequalities that have developed in the United States has run aground on some of the same obstacles that undermined regimes based on hereditary privilege. Families have found a variety of ways to engage in what policy researcher Richard Reeves calls "opportunity hoarding," the accumulation of privileges that enhance the probability that one's descendant will be able to successfully compete — even if this means the proverbial "being born on third base believing one has hit a triple." Reeves has no expectation that parents won't do what they can to better the lives of their children, but he does think "we should want to get rid of policies that allow parents to give their children an unfair advantage and in the process restrict the opportunities of others." Zoning laws, local fundraising to increase the budgets of neighborhood schools, college application gaming — all these help families to create a glass floor for themselves that becomes someone else's glass ceiling.[28] But it's very hard to convince parents that their efforts to protect their own are actually disadvantaging other people.

In debates about inequality, students are in the crosshairs of competing visions of how to construct a more just society. Students didn't create an economic system that seems geared to pay for increased productivity with ever-greater inequality, but many of the anxieties about these inequalities are projected onto students and the institutions that teach them. On many campuses, students themselves push back against a system that creates winners and losers, often by bringing riches to the wealthy. That explains why many young people are so alert to how their peers leverage privilege, or how their institutions reinforce hierarchies through prejudice. Young people for centuries have been at the forefront of resisting "the establishment," and it is no wonder that those who want to protect existing practices often turn against students and their teachers for their failure to appreciate the world their elders have built.

Few want to see themselves as the sorted object of a sorting machine. To be only the object of forces beyond oneself excludes the possibility of what Kant described as enlightenment — throwing off self-imposed immaturity. This is a process, after all, of developing agency. The modern idea of the student that we have been tracing is an idea of people *coming into their own* and not merely being assigned (or pushed into) a slot. Good students are those who learn to learn on their own, even without the presence of a teacher and even without immediate rewards.

In the 2020s, as learning modalities have proliferated with the internet and digital technologies, the word *student* has seemed too narrow to encompass the people of all ages who are learning new skills and seeking new experiences, often far away from traditional college campuses. Many educators who have been reimagining the classroom think "student" connotes immaturity and/or implies a delimited field of studies distinct from the new tech-savvy, adventurous learning that happens, in particular, in digital spaces. Active learning, or what some call "action learning," is meant to keep people from becoming "grinds," working only for the instructor's approval. They learn by doing things on their own initiative. This initiative is what the educator prizes. Take, for example, a teacher who writes that students in her classroom are only interested in "playing the game" to get a good grade. For her, "The word 'student' connotes compliance and external form more than anything intrinsic or enduring."[29] Students, we hear, are compelled by authorities or rules, while genuine learners are more authentically curious.[30] In this reframing, the student is too interested in being obedient to ever make progress in enlightenment. As a teacher writes in *Psychology Today:*

> Good students are those who understand what is being
> asked of them and who have the basic cognitive capability,
> socioemotional disposition, and willingness to meet those
> expectations. These individuals are task-oriented and

goal-directed, where the tasks are externally determined and the goals are getting the grades or passing the tests. . . . Good learners, by comparison, not only perform as well as good students, but they also have additional cognitive, social, and emotional characteristics. . . . For one, they enjoy learning for its own sake. . . . In effect, while good students are relatively skilled at information management, good learners are actively engaged in knowledge building.[31]

As educator and consultant Kathleen McClaskey puts it unironically in a message to teachers in "Learner vs Student: Who Do You Want in Your Classroom?": "Learners can learn without teachers, but students are only students when they have teachers."[32]

The word *learner* is meant to describe a certain kind of student – a really good one who displays autonomy indicating self-motivated inquiry and reflection. Perhaps most important, the preference for "learner" over "student" indicates that the teacher wants to work with someone who is active in acquiring knowledge or engaging in inquiry. This dovetails with the emergence over the last twenty years or more of project-based learning (PBL). As with learner versus student, the contrast between project-based instruction and traditional teaching hinges on activity versus passivity. From the PBL perspective, in the traditional college classroom the professor is a "sage on the stage" who dispenses wisdom that his students soak in as best they can (without falling asleep). In PBL's active-learning modalities, students learn by doing. This can seem pretty trivial: an instructor will ask large groups of learners short-answer questions that allow them to respond to electronic polls in the classroom. One can then see where one's answers fell in relation to other people in the class. Some instructors create small prizes or certificates for students who click on the right buttons to show they understand material. Rudimentary gamification seems to keep people on pace for the learning goals of the course. Teams with specific projects also work well with many students whose learning is energized through collaboration on tasks that results in some tangible result. In completing the task, they grasp abstract ideas, build skills, and gain real-world experience. By being active learners, to go back to Kant's formula, they are throwing off the kind of immaturity that comes from just absorbing someone else's lessons. By applying ideas to specific projects in concert with others, they are taking on responsibilities as they learn. Lessons actively acquired stick more. Research in STEM fields seems to confirm the power of active learning.[33] Still, many veteran college teachers are loath to try teaching approaches different from the ones they experienced as students, and many undergraduates are resistant to active learning.[34] Some protest against being assigned to teams that are uncongenial; others say they prefer to really focus on a lecture rather than being bombarded with multiple-choice questions to which they respond on their phones. Although the research shows that people learn more in project-based classes, students often object that it's a lot more work!

The active education envisioned by many scholars today is not individually oriented: it emphasizes cohort building. When University of North Carolina sociologist Tressie McMillan Cottom was building her digital sociology program, she was very conscious that students were learning to work together even as they learned sociological theory. One of the best ways to enhance prospects for degree completion is to create small communities of learners who are invested in their mutual success. "Everything is geared to be as constructivist as possible," she writes, "where the sociology theory they read connects to their own life and work experiences and vice versa." Professor and educational theorist Cathy Davidson recounts that the City University of New York's Accelerated Study in Associate Programs (ASAP) has more than doubled graduation rates at community colleges in New York City by recognizing and activating the various communities to which economically challenged students belong.[35] These programs emphasize that people are better students when they are not learning alone. The idea of the individual, autonomous student is replaced by the learner who is productively entangled, included, in community.

As many reimagine the new college student in technology-enhanced classrooms where project-based teams work on real-world problems rather than listen to a lecturer behind a lectern, it is worthwhile to recall a more traditional form of active learning: the small-group discussion of a text. In the seminars devoted to great books or a core curriculum, the point is not to train experts in ancient philosophy or Renaissance literature. The goal is to have students activate their own critical and creative capacities in relation to a work that has endured. In discussions, students don't just receive wisdom from a sage on the stage — they jointly explore issues that might help them construct more meaningful lives. Yale professor Anthony Kronman writes of the authentic "ethic of conversation" in seminars while bemoaning in Bloom-like fashion what he sees as a tide of democratic mediocrity among students more concerned with equality and diversity than excellence. Kronman thinks *some* people are capable of active learning in concert with one another, especially when they are faced with the enduring questions of the Western tradition.[36] Roosevelt Montás agrees about the ethic of the seminar devoted to canonical texts, but he emphasizes its democratizing potential. Actively learning in small discussion groups can be liberating for those, like himself, who come to the university from impoverished backgrounds. As Montás puts it, a classroom like this "looks to the meaning of a human life beyond the requirements of subsistence – instead of asking how to make a living, liberal education asks what living is for." In his book *Rescuing Socrates*, he gives an account of how the traditional great books seminar, part of the core curriculum at Columbia University, changed his life when he was still adjusting to being a poor immigrant in New York City, and how this kind of experience is "the most powerful tool we have to subvert the hierarchies of social privilege." Montás remains devoted to canonical texts he encountered as a student while recognizing that any canon must always be open to revision. The goal of the seminars is not to transmit knowledge of classics to students preparing for exams. Through "the active and engaged participation of each member of the group that constitutes a Core class knowledge is not transmitted from teacher to student but constructed by the group through a shared process of inquiry and reflection."[37] The construction of knowledge through active participation is key to both the traditional discussion session in a great books seminar and the PBL learning of the technologically enhanced "flipped classroom," a classroom where you do your homework with a team and watch recorded lectures on your own time.

The goal of creating a classroom of active learners – whether they are collaborating on a project or working through a text together to see how it might be relevant to their lives – is very close to the goal that Kant articulated for enlightenment. It is to leave behind immaturity and take responsibility for one's learning. Students are in the process of becoming active, of coming into maturity, and yet the goal of maturity cannot be decisively fixed in advance. There are many ways of learning freedom. The student is in a *not yet* phase, a time of ripening. Kant said that we lived not in an enlightened age but in an age of enlightenment—a process of leaving behind the "conveniences" of immaturity. Philosophers of education like American John Dewey and Brazilian Paulo Freire share this process-oriented view of the student's path. Dewey saw the classroom as an incubator of democracy, a space in which students develop practices of independence that will eventually allow them to contribute to the public sphere. And Freire underscored that education is the development of a student's humanity, since a core dimension of being human is being free. For Freire, the practices of critical dialogue in the classroom help students unlearn oppression and develop their latent capacities for freedom. The dialogue he envisioned breaks down the hierarchical distinction between learner and instructor, replacing it with a more egalitarian picture of the joint construction of knowledge. Dewey and Freire have had enormous influence on educational practices in the United States, as has, more recently and more subtly, the Indian artist and philosopher Rabindranath Tagore. Tagore emphasized that active learning isn't just about empowering the student to do more or acquire more; it's also about expanding the student's capacity for feeling, especially for empathy. "We may become powerful by knowledge, but we attain fullness by sympathy."[38]

If "attaining fullness" demands more than expanding the student's intellectual capacities, it may also require *unlearning* habits of mind and heart that close one off to the world. Through critical thinking we reduce our dependence on faulty reasoning and strengthen our ability to resist being misled. This is firmly in the Socratic tradition. Teachers should help students determine what kinds of information are most reliable, what makes a good argument, and which kinds of fallacies are used to manipulate people. Educators differ about so many things, but there is a broad consensus on the importance of critical thinking. There's even a Foundation for Critical Thinking to make the case for "universal intellectual values that transcend subject matter divisions: clarity, accuracy, precision, consistency, relevance, sound evidence, good reasons, depth, breadth and fairness."[39] No matter the area of study, critical thinking enables us to be better students by questioning whether we really know what we think we know.

People are not, of course, swayed only by argument and evidence — we are also creatures of feeling, and our emotions can sometimes lead us toward celebration or to outrage, irrespective of evidence and argument. It feels good to belong to a group, and critical thinking alone will not turn students from the pleasures of groupthink, scapegoating, or resentment; reason alone never supplants sentiment. Students need critical feeling — practiced emotional alternatives to the satisfactions of outrage.[40] In the United States today, outrage is braided together with self-absorption, with the tendency to intensify group identification by finding outsiders one can detest. Students learn this quickly from those in authority. Among the intellectual set, outrage is sublimated into irony, allowing the chattering class to police the borders of its in-groups without overtly subscribing to their norms. One can humorously dismiss outsiders without seeming to hold any beliefs that prove one's own membership in any particular group. It's easier to criticize others for their naïve beliefs than it is to defend one's own commitments. This was, we might recall, Thrasymachus's complaint lodged against Socrates' ironic skepticism in Plato's *Republic*. "He gives no answer himself but pulls to pieces the answer of someone else." Today, this may be less intellectual humility than a fear of committing oneself to anything.

—

171

How to use critical feeling to dislodge these tendencies? Teachers do this all the time when we enthusiastically introduce works that students might find foreign or offensive, when, as Mark Edmundson puts it, we teach what we love.[41] We do this by using Shakespeare to expand their capacity for empathy, or when we use James Baldwin to deepen their understanding of racist betrayal.[42] When we help students to appreciate a character in a novel who is not wholly sympathetic, or to admire an argument even when it runs counter to their own assumptions, we are expanding their emotional as well as their intellectual registers. When our teaching invites students to occupy identities and ideologies they would never encounter in their own curated networks, we are enhancing their abilities to process the power of emotions.

When my students try to understand why Aristotle made his arguments about habit, why Rousseau saw inequality linked to the development of society, what Jane Austen meant by vanity as an obstacle to love, or why Toni Morrison's Sethe holds what haunts her, they are exercising their empathy and strengthening their power of generous insight. They are becoming more aware of how their feelings are aroused or redirected. In being willing to make emotional as well as intellectual connections to ideas and characters that disturb them, they broaden their worldviews. If we want our students to learn discernment and not just critique, we must give them more opportunities to wrestle with ideas and emotions that they wouldn't encounter on their own.[43]

Expanding the repertoire of feelings has long been part of what maturity means for a liberal education—feeling for oneself, not just thinking for oneself. Through history, literature, and the arts we make connections to worlds of emotion, creativity, and intelligence that take us beyond our individual identities and our group allegiances. The exercise of critical feeling should make students less susceptible to demagogic manipulation and to the misleading politics of resentment. It should make them more open to understanding why other people care about the things they do. By exploring the complexities of the world, students can practice making connections that are intellectual *and* affective. And in a political and cultural context that encourages crude parochialism under the guise of group solidarity, helping them do so through increasing their powers of critical feeling is more important than ever.

Strong teachers often provoke very powerful feelings, but the best teach in ways that eliminate the need for their teaching: "Your educators cannot go beyond being your liberators," said Friedrich Nietzsche in 1874. What one has to know to be a good art teacher, said John Baldessari about a century later, is when to get out of the way.[44] The goal of the teacher is to help the student be more than a spectator, more than a consumer of lessons. Strong teachers create an environment where everyone can become an active participant in the learning process. "Our deadness toward all but one particular kind of joy would thus be the price we inevitably have to pay for being practical creatures," William James wrote in an address to teachers. But when learning works, when the creative intelligence of students is animated, "then the whole scheme of our customary values gets confounded, then our self is riven and its narrow interests fly to pieces, then a new centre and a new perspective must be found."[45] Teachers have an obligation to introduce students to things about themselves and the world they are unlikely to find on their own, things that will help them build new perspectives, new modes of feeling. Teachers can help students get to a place where it is more likely that they'll find that new centering perspective, but part of leaving one's immaturity behind is finding that oneself. Long after official graduations, many students remain enormously grateful to the gifted teachers who opened up possibilities of inquiry and appreciation that might otherwise have never been discovered – teachers who also knew the right moments to get out of the way. It wasn't just that they knew things that students aspired to understand (although that can certainly be part of the picture); it's more that they had developed habits of paying attention, analysis, and openness that students want for themselves. Students don't merely learn to adopt their teachers' criteria of judgment so that they can evaluate the world from their mentors' perspective; teachers point students toward experiences and realities that become available through guidance. In being great teachers, they help those they work with become better students.

I first set foot on a campus almost fifty years ago, and I've spent most of my time since then working at different colleges. Over this period, the percentage of Americans who attend college has increased dramatically. Higher education has become an expectation for many Americans – the end goal of one's student years. As we bring this study of the idea of the student to a close, let's consider how one might choose a college in a way that makes the most out of being a person whose role it is to learn – how to make the most out of being a student. If students in general occupy a liminal space as they leave immaturity behind, college students in particular exist at the interstices between dependence and autonomy. Children are supposed to go where they are told, and in the West going to school through adolescence is generally a requirement. In the contemporary United States, many people find themselves excluded from earning a living wage if they don't have some form of college degree. This degree has come to symbolize one's maturation. Apprentices were said to "take the freedom" when they were no longer bound to the master of a trade and were ready to set up their own shops. Undergraduates taking their diplomas today are supposed to be free to be independent in the economy and society. If only that were always the case.

Young people preparing to attend college in many cases find themselves with what feels like a momentous choice: which school will provide the best combination of resources and challenges that will launch them into the adult world? Most students thinking about college in the United States will make this decision with economics in mind. How much will college cost, or which school is closer to home or a job? Most students who enroll in higher education in the United States attend community colleges, which, like European universities, are filled with undergraduates who commute to school and often have jobs even while they pursue their studies. The credentials community colleges offer and the skills they impart help many Americans build economically viable lives. Those thinking about going to school further from home often consider which school offers the most generous financial aid package. The prohibitive cost of higher education in the United States has been an issue of growing importance over the last twenty-five years or so. Even when I went to school in the 1970s, the costs were daunting, and I decided to graduate in three years to save my family some money. Colleges can be expensive to attend, and student indebtedness is a serious problem for millions of people. If one types the word *student* into Google's search engine, one of the first options sure to come up is "loans." It's hard to become an autonomous, enlightened adult when one is carrying around significant debt from one's student years.

For young people with the good fortune to be able to choose where to continue their education, no formula works for everyone. Given economic pressures, many students looking at colleges think they should pick the one that gives them the credentials that will land them the most highly paid job. This is a narrow (and ultimately impractical) vision of what higher education should provide. Sure, one should leave college with the ability to compete for gainful employment. But that first job should be the worst job you'll ever have, and your undergraduate years should prepare you for more than just immediate entry into the workforce.

A college education should prepare students to thrive by creating habits of mind and spirit that will continue to develop over a lifetime. Thriving means realizing your capabilities, which is a form of freedom. A liberal education should enable you to discover capabilities you didn't even know you had while deepening those that provide you with meaning and direction.[46] A strong college education, one infused with liberal learning, helps create what philosopher Martha Nussbaum has called "new spaces for diverse possibilities of flourishing."[47]

Discovering these possibilities for flourishing is the opposite of trying to figure out how to conform to the world as it is. Conforming is a losing proposition, as Emerson noted a century ago, not least because the world is changing so rapidly; tomorrow it won't be what it is today. When you flourish, you find ways of shaping change, not just coping with it. The students who get the most out of college are often anti-conformists aiming to discover who they are and what kind of work they will find meaningful. Over the years, I've often found them to be the most interesting people to have in my classes. Paradoxically, they also often turn out to be the people who add the greatest value to the organizations in which they work. The students who get the most out of college also expand the horizons and opportunities of those around them. They are empowered members of communities as well as skilled individuals.

—

When young people visit prospective colleges where they are trying to imagine themselves as students, they are encountering institutions with distinct yet labile personalities. It's the evolution of student culture over many years that comes to define the way a place feels to the young men and women who spend these transitional years on campus. It also helps launch them into what comes after college. Students — not teachers and officials — make that culture. America's most intellectually alive campuses are places that nurture and respond to the energies of their students. That's what students and their families are trying to understand when they visit. They want to feel this percolating force and to get a sense if this is the kind of energy that they can contribute to and be turned on by. When they feel that energetic compatibility, they are ready to make the choice.

Whatever choice students make about where to attend college, there are three things that they should learn while there. The first is to discover what they love to do. This isn't as easy as it may sound, for many young people mistake what they've been told they're good at with what they love to do. A teacher may have told the student, "You are really great at math!" or "You are an excellent reader of poetry!" but this kind of reinforcement should not distract the student from opportunities to try out new fields of study or methods of inquiry. College is the time to experiment in learning, a time to expose oneself to a variety of subject areas and practices to find out what kind of work brings one meaning, brings one joy.[48] When I was a student, I was fortunate enough to stumble into an introductory philosophy class and to have my mind filled with questions that were thrilling to explore. The combination of teacher and subject matter made me feel alive — alive with confusion, perhaps, but in a state of attentiveness that I have cherished.

—

The second thing that every student should learn wherever they go to college is to get better at whatever they love to do. It's not enough to "discover one's passion"; students should be inspired (and pushed) to develop practices through which they become more skillful. This requires hard work, and it requires teachers who help students grasp that they can develop further than they might have thought possible. I was fortunate enough to have teachers who challenged my arguments, urged me to read more widely and more deeply, and covered my papers in red pencil marks. Teachers must get over their fear of alienating students by setting high standards, and undergraduates must come to appreciate that being criticized is something to cherish — not something to defend oneself against. Students should also learn how to share their skills, knowledge, or wisdom with others. That's the third thing everyone should learn, whatever school they attend. Students who get the most out of college are able to translate what they've learned on campus to people beyond its borders.

The choice of a college today in the United States isn't just about "fit" and "comfort," and it certainly shouldn't be reduced to the prestige of the school or the amenities it offers. The choice should reflect one's aspirations, where one can imagine oneself discovering more about the world and one's capacities to interact with it. The college one chooses should be a place at which one can thrive, finding out so much more about oneself as one also discovers important dimensions of the world.

College has become a vital place in our culture to develop the appetite for lifelong learning, but it's hardly the only place. Those who followed Confucius never believed they would be done learning, but they did believe there were certain ways of interacting with tradition and with the world around them that were more conducive to understanding their place in it. Socrates reminded his interlocutors that ignorance wasn't something one ever fully left behind, and that a spirit of inquiry and intellectual humility made for a life worth living – and a polity worth living in. The disciples of Jesus looked to their teacher to find the path to follow, to learn to cultivate in themselves the compassion that would prepare them for the world to come. The great teachers were themselves never done being students. They exemplified what it means always to be on a path of enlightenment, as Kant said, but never enlightened. These are the kinds of people who activate wonder, a capacity for appreciation, and a taste for inquiry. These kinds of people, these perpetual students, aim not at completion but at an open-ended practice that brings joy and meaning. Over the course of a lifetime, they are good company to keep.

NOTES

INTRODUCTION

1. See Sylvia Goodman, "Researchers Did a Deep Dive into Efforts to Restrict Critical Race Theory. Here's What They Found," *Chronicle of Higher Education*, August 3, 2022. Goodman draws on this database: https://crtforward.law.ucla.edu/.

CHAPTER 1. ICONIC TEACHERS, EXEMPLARY STUDENTS

1. Confucius, *The Analects: An Online Teaching Translation*, trans. Robert Eno (2015), 18:4 (p. 100), https://chinatxt.sitehost.iu.edu/Analects_of_Confucius_(Eno-2015).pdf.

2. Ibid., 1:1 (p. 1).

3. See Klaus Mühlhand, *The Making of Modern China: From Great Qing to Xi Jinping* (Cambridge, MA: Harvard University Press, 2019), xx.

4. See Stephen C. Angle, *Sagehood: The Contemporary Significance of Neo-Confucian Philosophy* (Oxford: Oxford University Press, 2009), 35.

5. See Amy Olberding, "The Consummation of Sorrow: An Analysis of Confucius' Grief for Yan Hui," *Philosophy East and West* 54, no. 3 (2004). "Confucius' models are often cultural heroes, and shifts in culture may engender a need for models that more readily resonate with the new context of a new audience" (282).

6. Confucius, *Analects*, 5:4 (p. 18). The passage on junzis not being vessels is 2:12 (p. 6).

7. Ibid., 1:15 (p. 4).

8. Ibid., 5:12 (p. 20).

9. Amy Olberding, *Moral Exemplars in the Analects: The Good Person Is That* (New York: Routledge, 2002), 166.

10. Confucius, *Analects*, 7:11 (p. 31), 11:22 (p. 55), 5:7 (pp. 18–19).

11. Ibid., 17:8 (p. 96).

---

12. Ibid., 6:3 (p. 24), 11:4 (p. 52), 2:9 (p. 6). The translation of the last quote has been altered.

13. Ibid., 11:10 (p. 53).

14. Ibid., 9:11 (p. 41). Translation altered.

15. Annping Chin, *The Authentic Confucius: A Life of Thought and Politics* (New York: Scribner, 2007), 145, 150.

16. Xenophon, *Memorabilia*, book IV, chap. 7, p. 1. A readily available edition can be found at https://philocyclevl.files.wordpress.com/2016/09/xenophon-memorabilia-or-the-recollections-cornell.pdf.

17. Ibid., book III, chap. 19, p. 3.

18. Ibid., book III, chap. 11, p. 1.

19. Ibid., book III, chap. 11.

20. Ibid., book III, chap. 13.

21. Ibid.

22. Plato, *Apology*, in *The Complete Works*, ed. John M. Cooper (Indianapolis: Hackett, 1997), 20.

23. Ibid., 22, 30. Translation of the last quotation is modified.

24. Plato, *Republic*, in *The Complete Works*," 982. Translation of the first quotation is modified.

25. Alexander Nehamas, *The Art of Living: Socratic Reflections from Plato to Foucault* (Berkeley: University of California Press, 2000), 40.

26. Ibid., 44.

27. Plato, *Republic*, 1136.

28. Of course, the allegory of the cave is at the heart of a work on justice, a dialogue concerned with the ideal state. Those who are turned away from the shadows and toward the good, away from the senses and toward the realm of ideas, are to be the leaders of the city. They will do so with some reluctance for "a city whose prospective rulers are least eager to rule must of necessity be most free from civil war." Ibid., 1137.

29. Plato, *Apology*, 21–22.

30. Ibid., 35.

31. Ibid., 28, 34–35.

CHAPTER 2. CHILDREN, APPRENTICES, STUDENTS

1. Philippe Ariès, *Centuries of Childhood: A Social History of Family Life* (New York: Knopf, 1962). Ariès's conclusions would be supported by English historians like Peter Laslett and then Lawrence Stone. Stone argued that it wasn't until well into the early modern period that families moved from a stage of indifference about their young relations to one of affection. See his *The Family, Sex and Marriage in England, 1500–1800* (Charlottesville: University of Virginia Press, 1977).

2. Barbara A. Hanawalt, *"Of Good and Ill Repute"*: *Gender and Social Control in Medieval England* (Oxford: Oxford University Press, 1998), ProQuest Ebook Central, http://ebookcentral.proquest.com/lib/wesleyan/detail.action?docID= 4701349.

3. Generalizations are bound to miss a lot, but 40 percent mortality before ten years old is not a bad estimate in the medieval period or even into the sixteenth century. Less than half of children made it past twenty. See Nicholas Orme, *Medieval Children* (New Haven, CT: Yale University Press, 2001), 113.

4. Nicholas Orme, "Children in Medieval England," in *Childhood in History: Perceptions of Children in the Ancient and Medieval Worlds* (London: Routledge, 2018), 328.

5. See Daniel T. Kline, introduction to *Medieval Literature for Children* (London: Taylor and Frances, 2003).

6. Hanawalt, *"Of Good and Ill Repute,"* 160.

7. Shulamith Shahar, *Childhood in the Middle Ages* (New York: Routledge, 1990), 101.

8. See, for example, Hugh Cunningham, *Children and Childhood in Western Society since 1500* (New York: Pearson, Longman, 2005), 83-86.

9. Hanawalt, *"Of Good and Ill Repute,"* 177.

10. Though there were apprenticeships for girls in some trades. See D. L. Simonton, "Apprenticeship: Training and Gender in Eighteenth-Century England," in *Markets and Manufacture in Early Industrial Europe,* ed. Maxine Berg (London: Routledge, 1991), 227-58.

11. Hanawalt, *"Of Good and Ill Repute,"* 182.

12. Ibid., 190.

13. Keith Thomas puts it nicely in saying that young people had "a casual attitude to private property, an addiction to mischief, and a predilection for what most adults regarded as noise and dirt." See his "Children in Early Modern England," in *Children and Their Books,* ed. G. Avery and J. Briggs (Oxford: Oxford University Press, 1989), 57, quoted in Cunningham, *Children and Childhood,* 98.

14. See Rahikainen Marjatta, *Centuries of Child Labor: European Experiences from the Seventeenth Century to the Twentieth Century* (New York: Routledge, 2004), 5-6.

15. Pamela H. Smith, *The Body of the Artisan: Art and Experience in the Scientific Revolution* (Chicago: University of Chicago Press, 2004), 7-8.

16. See Jacob F. Field, "Apprenticeship Migration to London from the North-east of England in the Seventeenth Century," *London Journal* 35, no. 1 (2010): 1-21.

17. Ibid., 14.

18. See Laura Gowing, *Ingenious Trade: Women and Work in Seventeenth-Century London* (London: Cambridge University Press, 2021). The precedents and subsequent developments are discussed in Stephanie R. Hovland, "Girls as Apprentices in Later Medieval London," in *London and the Kingdom: Essays in Honour of Caroline M. Barron*, ed. Matthew Davies and Andrew Prescott (Donington, UK: Paul Watkins, 2008), 179–94; Marjorie Keniston McIntosh, *Working Women in English Society, 1300–1620* (Cambridge: Cambridge University Press, 2005); I. K. Ben-Amos and Ilana Krausman, "Women Apprentices in the Trade and Crafts of Early Modern Bristol," *Continuity and Change* 6, no. 2 (August 1991): 227–52; Keith Snell, *Annals of the Labouring Poor: Social Change and Agrarian England, 1660–1900* (Cambridge: Cambridge University Press, 1987), chap. 6; Joan Lane, *Apprenticeship in England, 1600–1914* (New York: Routledge, 1996); Deborah Simonton, "Apprenticeship: Training and Gender in Eighteenth-Century England," in Berg, *Markets and Manufacture in Early Industrial Europe*. For a European parallel, see Danielle van der Heuvel, "Guilds, Gender Policies and Economic Opportunities for Women in Early Modern Dutch Towns," in *Female Agency in the Urban Economy: Gender in European Towns, 1640–1830,* ed. Anne Montenach and Deborah Simonton (New York: Routledge, 2013), 116–33.

19. See Jan deVries, *The Industrious Revolution: Consumer Behavior and the Household Economy, 1650 to the Present* (Cambridge: Cambridge University Press, 2008); and Laura Gowing, "Girls on Forms: Apprenticing Young Women in Seventeenth-Century London," *Journal of British Studies* 55, no. 3 (2016): 447–73, doi:10.1017/jbr.2016.54.

20. Amy Louise Erickson, "Eleanor Mosley and Other Milliners in the City of London Companies, 1700–1750," *History Workshop Journal* 71 (2001): 147–72.

21. Ibid., 164.

22. Jean-Jacques Rousseau, quoted in Alan Downing, "The Last Cabinotier of Saint Gervais: The Horological Curiosity in the Historic Centre of Geneva Watchmaking," *WatchesbySJX.com*, November 9, 2020, https://watchesbysjx.com/2020/11/bruno-pesenti-geneva-watchmaker.html, from Daniel Palmieri and Irène Herrmann, *Faubourg Saint-Gervais, mythes retrouvés* (Geneva: Slatkine, 1995).

23. Jean-Jacques Rousseau, *Confessions*, trans. Angela Scholar (Oxford: Oxford University Press, 2000), 31. Translation modified.

24. Ibid., 30.

25. Ibid., 42.

26. Franklin discusses this period of his life in *Autobiography of Benjamin Franklin*, ed. Frank Woodworth Pine (New York: Henry Holt, 1916), chap. 2, https://www.gutenberg.org/files/20203/20203-h/20203-h.htm#I. See also Walter Isaacson, *Benjamin Franklin: An American Life* (New York: Simon and Schuster, 2003), 5–35.

27. See the Library of Congress exhibition *Franklin in His Own Words*, https://www.loc.gov/exhibits/franklin/franklin-printer.html.

28. Orme, *Medieval Children*, 129ff.

29. See "The Protestant Education in the 16th Century," *Musée protestant*, n.d., https://museeprotestant.org/en/notice/the-protestant-education-in-the-xvith-century/.

30. Cunningham, *Children and Childhood*, 120–21.

31. Wesley is quoted by historian Allison P. Coudert, "Educating Girls in Early Modern Europe and America," in *Childhood in the Middle Ages and the Renaissance: The Results of a Paradigm Shift in the History of Mentality*, ed. Albrecht Classen (Berlin: Walter de Gruyter, 2005), 394. Coudert goes on to say, "The whole weight of evangelical parental discipline was directed at breaking a child's will" (394).

32. Quoted in ibid., 395.

33. See Robert Axtel, *Wisdom's Workshop: The Rise of the Modern University* (Princeton, NJ: Princeton University Press, 2016), 7.

34. Jacques Verger, *Les universités au Moyen Âge* (Paris: Presses Universitaires de France, 1973); Verger, "Patterns," in *A History of the University in Europe*, vol. 1: *Universities in the Middle Ages*, ed. Hilde De Ridder-Symoens (Cambridge: Cambridge University Press, 1992), 35–67. See also Axtel, *Wisdom's Workshop*, chaps. 1 and 2.

35. Henry Louis Gates Jr., "Writing 'Race' and the Difference It Makes," in *"Race," Writing, and Difference* (Chicago: University of Chicago Press, 1992). See also Andrew S. Curran, *The Anatomy of Blackness: Science and Slavery in the Age of Enlightenment* (Baltimore, MD: Johns Hopkins University Press, 2011), 118. See also the introduction to the recent volume edited by Gates and Curran, *Who's Black and Why: A Hidden Chapter in the 18th Century Invention of Race* (Cambridge, MA: Harvard University Press, 2022). The Hume quotation is discussed in this volume on p. 41.

36. See *Slaves and Free Persons of Color: An Act, Documenting the American South*, https://docsouth.unc.edu/nc/slavesfree/slavesfree.html#:~:text=If%20any%20slave%20shall%20teach,his%20or%20her%20bare%20back.

37. *The Poems of Phillis Wheatley*, rev. ed., ed. Julian D. Mason (Chapel Hill: University of North Carolina Press, 1989), 52, 171. See also *The Poetry Foundation*, https://www.poetryfoundation.org/poets/phillis-wheatley#tab-poems.

38. See Wheatley to Occum (1774), *The Poetry Foundation*, https://www.poetryfoundation.org/poets/phillis-wheatley#tab-poems. A few years after her manumission, Wheatley married a free black man, John Peters. It was a time of political unrest and economic dislocation in North America, and the Peters household fell on hard times. Phillis continued to write, but poverty and disease took their toll. The poet was thirty-one when she died.

39. Quoted by David W. Blight, *Frederick Douglass: Prophet of Freedom* (New York: Simon and Schuster, 2018), 39.

40. See Heather Andrea Williams, *Self-Taught: African American Education in Slavery and Freedom* (Chapel Hill: University of North Carolina Press, 2005), 20.

41. Kabria Baumgartner, "*Incidents in the Life of a Slave Girl*, Education and Abolition," *Ethnic Studies Review* 32, no. 2 (2009): 57.

42. See Jarvis R. Givens, *Fugitive Pedagogy: Carter G. Woodson and the Art of Black Teaching* (Cambridge, MA: Harvard University Press, 2021). Givens sees black education more generally as an act of resistance against slavery and white supremacy, what he calls a "fugitive" tradition.

43. Frederick Douglass, "What to the Slave, Is the Fourth of July" (1852), *National Museum of African American History & Culture*, https://nmaahc.si.edu/explore/stories/nations-story-what-slave-fourth-july.

CHAPTER 3. THE EMERGENCE OF THE MODERN STUDENT

1. Kant, "What Is Enlightenment?" (1784), See https://resources.saylor.org/wwwresources/archived/site/wp-content/uploads/2011/02/What-is-Enlightenment.pdf. "Immaturity" and "tutelage" are translations of Kant's *Unmündigkeit*.

2. Ibid.

3. *Kant in the Classroom*, https://users.manchester.edu/facstaff/ssnaragon/kant/Home/index.htm. See also Ernst Cassirer, *Kant's Life and Thought*, trans. James Haden (New Haven, CT: Yale University Press, 1981), 15.

4. Charles Rollin, *The Method of Teaching and Studying the Belles Lettres*, vol. 4 (London, A. Betteworth and C. Hitch, 1734), 203, https://books.google.com/books?id=ttpCAQAAMAAJ&pg=PA203&lpg=PA203&dq=rollin,+%.

5. Charles Salas, "The Punic Wars in France and Britain" (PhD diss., Claremont Graduate School, 1996). Rollin quotations from "Dicours sur l'instruction gratuite," cited in Albert Charles Gaudin, *The Educational Views of Charles Rollin* (New York: Columbia University Press, 1939), 15–18.

6. Rollin, *Ancient History*, 2:337, quoted by Mark W. Graham, "Charles Rollins and Universal History in America," *Journal of Modern History* 17, no. 2 (2018): 343.

7. See the English-language version of the *Encyclopédie* archived by the University of Michigan: https://quod.lib.umich.edu/d/did/.

8. See Andrew Curran, *Diderot: The Art of Thinking Freely* (New York: Other Press, 2018).

9. Faiguet's entry on studies can be found at Robert Morrissey and Glenn Roe, eds., *Research and Archival Materials, University of Chicago: ARTFL Encyclopédie Project* (Autumn 2022), https://artflsrv03.uchicago.edu/philologic4/encyclopedie1117/navigate/6/324/.

10. Denis Diderot, "Learn," in *The Encyclopedia of Diderot & d'Alembert Collaborative Translation Project,* trans. Malcolm Eden (Ann Arbor: Michigan Publishing,

University of Michigan Library, 2010), http://hdl.handle.net/2027/spo. did2222.0001.212. Originally published as "Apprendre," in *Encyclopédie ou dictionnaire raisonné des sciences, des arts et des métiers* (Paris, 1751), 1:555.

11. Jean-Baptiste le Rond d'Alembert, "School, Philosophy of the," in *The Encyclopedia of Diderot & d'Alembert Collaborative Translation Project*, trans. Jennifer Popiel (Ann Arbor: Michigan Publishing, University of Michigan Library, 2003), http://hdl.handle.net/2027/spo.did2222.0000.025. Originally published as "Ecole, philosophie de l'," in *Encyclopédie ou dictionnaire raisonné des sciences, des arts et des métiers* (Paris, 1755), 5:303-4.

12. Diderot, "Learn."

13. Jean-Jacques Rousseau, *Emile; or, On Education* (New York: Basic Books, 1979), 34.

14. Ibid., 376.

15. Mary Wollstonecraft, *A Vindication of the Rights of Men and a Vindication of the Rights of Woman* (Cambridge: Cambridge University Press, 1995), 90.

16. Ibid., 251, quoted in Sylvana Tomaselli, *Mary Wollstonecraft: Philosophy, Passion and Politics* (Princeton, NJ: Princeton University Press, 2021), 79. See also Wollstonecraft's 1787 publication *Notes on the Education of Daughters* (Cambridge: Cambridge University Press, 2014), 85.

17. M. Reuter, " 'Like a Fanciful Kind of Half Being': Mary Wollstonecraft's Criticism of Jean-Jacques Rousseau," *Hypatia* 29, no. 4 (2014): 925-41. See also Sandrine Bergès, *The Routledge Guidebook to Wollstonecraft's "A Vindication of the Rights of Woman"* (London: Routledge, 2013).

18. Tomaselli, *Mary Wollstonecraft*, 179.

19. Although extracts from the text circulated among education reformers for decades, it was published only in 1896. On the relation of Humboldt's initiatives and those of Friedrich Schleiermacher, see Paul Reitter and Chad Wellmon, *Permanent Crisis: The Humanities in a Disenchanted Age* (Chicago: University of Chicago Press, 2021), 58-60.

20. Louis Menand, Paul Reitter, and Chad Wellmon, eds., *The Rise of the Research University: A Sourcebook* (Chicago, University of Chicago Press, 2017), 105.

21. See Andrea Wulf, *The Invention of Nature: Alexander von Humboldt's New World* (New York: Vintage, 2015).

22. Wilhelm von Humboldt, "On the Internal and External Organization of the Higher Scientific Institutions in Berlin" (1809), *German History in Documents and Images*, https://ghdi.ghi-dc.org/sub_document.cfm?document_id=3642.

23. Ibid.

24. Humboldt, quoted by Malte Brinkman, "Humboldt's Theory of Bildung as Embodied Bildung: An Attempt," *Research Gate*, October 2019, https://www.researchgate.net/profile/MalteBrinkmann/publication/336638107_Humboldts_Theory_of_Bildung_as_Embodied_Bildung_an_Attempt/links/5da91650a6

fdccc99d911d75/Humboldt-s-Theory-of-Bildung-as-Embodied-Bildung-an-At
tempt.pdf.

25. David Sorkin, "Wilhelm Von Humboldt: The Theory and Practice of
Self-Formation (Bildung), 1791–1810," *Journal of the History of Ideas* 44, no. 1
(1983): 63.

26. Ibid., 69.

27. George Ticknor, *Life, Letters and Journals* (Boston: James R. Osgood,
1876), 91.

28. Ibid., 98.

29. James Morgan Hart, *German Universities: A Narrative of Personal Experience, Together with Recent Statistical Information, Practical Suggestions, and a Comparison of the German, English and American Systems of Higher Education* (New York: Putnam, 1874), v.

30. Hart also stressed that even small provincial schools in Germany were superior to almost any high school one could find in the United States. See ibid.,
277–78.

31. Quotations on dueling from Hart are from ibid., 79, 73, 67.

32. Ibid., 289, 287, 288.

33. Humboldt, in Menand, Reitter, and Wellmon, *The Rise of the Research University*, 112.

34. Hart, *German Universities*, 291, 274.

35. Ibid., 290, 295.

36. Thomas Jefferson to Thaddeus Koscisko, quoted in Lorraine Smith Pangle
and Thomas L. Pangle, *The Learning of Liberty: The Educational Ideas of the American
Founders* (Lawrence: University of Kansas Press), 108.

37. Thomas Jefferson, Rockfish Report, in *Crusade against Ignorance: Thomas Jefferson on Education*, ed. Gordon Lee (New York: Teachers College Press, 1961), 119.

38. Ralph Waldo Emerson, "The School," in *The Early Lectures of Ralph Waldo
Emerson* (Cambridge, MA: Harvard University Press, 1959), 48. Also at *American
Transcendentalism Web*, https://archive.vcu.edu/english/engweb/transcendental
ism/authors/emerson/essays/education.html.

39. Ralph Waldo Emerson, "The American Scholar," in *Selected Writings of Emerson*, ed. Donald McQuade (New York: Modern Library, 1981), 51.

40. Ralph Waldo Emerson, "Celebration of Intellect," in *The Complete Works of
Ralph Waldo Emerson*, vol. 12: *Natural History of the Intellect and Other Papers* (New
York: Houghton Mifflin, 1904), https://quod.lib.umich.edu/e/emerson/495710
7.0012.001/132:7?page=root;size=100;view=image.

41. Emerson, "An Address," in *The Early Lectures*, 199.

42. Emerson, "The Divinity School Address," in *Selected* Writings, 112, 110.
On Emerson's aversive thinking, see Stanley Cavell, *Conditions Handsome and
Unhandsome: The Constitution of Emersonian Perfectionism* (Chicago: University of
Chicago Press, 1990), chap. 1.

43. Emerson, "The American Scholar," 56.

44. See Robert D. Richardson, *Emerson: The Mind on Fire* (Berkeley: University of California Press, 1995), 265.

45. Emerson, "The American Scholar," 49.

46. Emerson, "Circles," in *Selected Writings*, 272.

CHAPTER 4. THE STUDENT IN COLLEGE

1. Derrick P. Alridge and Dorothy Strickland, *The Educational Thought of W.E.B. Du Bois: An Intellectual History* (New York: Teachers College Press, 2008), *ProQuest Ebook Central*, http://ebookcentral.proquest.com/lib/wesleyan/detail.action?docID=5405739.

2. David Levering Lewis, *W.E.B. Du Bois: Biography of a Race, 1868–1919* (New York: Henry Holt, 1993), 60.

3. Ibid., 61.

4. *Fisk Herald* 5, no. 10 (June 1888), https://hbcudigitallibrary.auctr.edu/digital/collection/FUPP/id/1328/rec/4.

5. Lewis, *Du Bois: Biography of a Race*, 92; W.E.B. Du Bois, *The Autobiography of W.E.B. Du Bois* (New York: International, 1968), 129–34.

6. See Lewis, *Du Bois*, 92; and W.E.B. Du Bois, "A Negro Student at Harvard at the End of the 19th Century," *Massachusetts Review* 1, no. 3 (Spring 1960), https://www.massreview.org/sites/default/files/Du%20Bois%2C%20WEB.pdf.

7. David Leight, "Letters to a Former President," *Humanities*, July 2019, https://www.neh.gov/article/letters-former-president.

8. David Levering Lewis, *W.E.B. Du Bois: A Biography, 1868–1963* (New York: Henry Holt, 2009), 92–95; Anthony Appiah, *Lines of Descent: W.E.B. Du Bois and the Emergence of* Identity (Cambridge, MA: Harvard University Press, 2014), 11–12.

9. Kenneth Barkin, "W.E.B. Du Bois' Love Affair with Imperial Germany," *German Studies Review* 28, no. 2 (May 2005): 285–302. Barkin's hypothesis was that Du Bois's acceptance in Imperial Germany was in great part due to the way he dressed: "In the Germany of the 1890s dress trumped race" (297). Appiah comments that he was "a bit of a dandy" (*Lines of Descent*, 12).

10. Lewis, *Du Bois: A Biography, 1868–1963*, 129.

11. Barkin, "W.E.B. Du Bois' Love Affair," 297.

12. Michelle Rief, "Rural Black Woman as Deliverer: Margaret Murray Washington, Her Vision and Life's Work," *Alexander Street* (2015), 2. See also Laurie Wilkie, *An Archaeology of Mothering: An African American Midwife's Tale* (New York: Routledge, 2003), 182–83.

13. "The Tuskegee Woman's Club, written by Margaret Murray Washington, 1865–1925," *Southern Workman,* 49, no. 8 (August 1920): 365–69, cited by Rief, "Rural Black Woman," 7.

14. Louise W. Knight, *Jane Addams: Spirit in Action* (New York: Norton, 2010), 76.

15. Ibid., 85–88.

16. On Smith College, see Helen Lefkowitz Horowitz, *Alma Mater: Design and Experience in the Women's Colleges from Their 19th Century Beginnings to the 1930s* (New York: Knopf, 1984).

17. Horowitz emphasizes that the Smith founders harbored fears of intense female friendships of the kind they thought unnatural that were found in women's schools like Vassar. Ibid., 75.

18. Ibid., 80.

19. Robert J. Sprague, "Education and Race Suicide," *Journal of Heredity* 6 (May 1915): 231–32, quoted in Horowitz, *Alma Mater,* 280.

20. Horowitz, *Alma Mater,* 289.

21. Ibid., 284. See also Lynn Peril, *College Girl: Bluestockings, Sex Kittens and Co-eds Then and Now* (New York: Norton, 2006), chap. 2.

22. See Steven J. Novak, *The Rights of Youth: American Colleges and Student Revolt, 1798–1815* (Cambridge, MA: Harvard University Press, 2013), chap. 2.

23. Frederick Rudolph, "Neglect of Students as a Historical Tradition," in *The College and the Student: An Assessment of Relationships and Responsibilities in Undergraduate Education by Administrators, Faculty Members, and Public Officials,* ed. Lawrence E. Dennis and Joseph F. Kauffman (Washington, DC: American Council on Education, 1966), 47.

24. See Gerald Graff, *Professing Literature: An Institutional History* (Chicago: University of Chicago Press, 2007), 25.

25. Michael Hevel, "A Historiography of College Students 30 Years After Helen Horowitz's *Campus Life,*" in *Higher Education: Handbook of Theory and Research,* vol. 32, ed. Michael B. Paulsen (Springer, 2017), 431. Hevel is summarizing D. G. McGuigan, *A Dangerous Experiment: 100 Years of Women at the University of Michigan* (Ann Arbor, MI: Center for the Continuing Education of Women, 1970).

26. Andrew Delbanco, *College: What It Was Is and Should Be* (Princeton, NJ: Princeton University Press, 2014), 54.

27. Helen Lefkowitz Horowitz, *Campus Life: Undergraduate Cultures from the End of the 18th Century to the Present* (New York: Knopf, 1987), 14.

28. Lyman Bagg, quoted in Graff, *Professing Literature,* 26.

29. Graff, *Professing Literature,* 33.

30. Daniel A. Clark, *Creating the College Man: American Mass Magazines and Middle-Class Manhood, 1890–1915* (Madison: University of Wisconsin Press, 2010).

31. Groups of men excluded from traditional fraternities started their own organizations. Some became quite powerful. See, for example, Alpha Phi Alpha as portrayed in the collection Gregory S. Parks and Stefan M. Bradley, eds., *Alpha Phi Alpha: A Legacy of Greatness* (Lexington: University Press of Kentucky, 2012).

32. Hevel, "Historiography," 473.

33. Clark, *Creating the College Man.*

34. Horowitz, *Campus Life,* 202.

35. See Daniel A. Clark, "The Two Joes Meet — Joe College, Joe Veteran: The GI Bill, College Education, and Postwar American Culture," *History of Education Quarterly* 38, no. 2 (1998): 165–90.

36. David Potts, *Wesleyan University, 1910–1970: Academic Ambition and Middle-Class America* (Middletown, CT: Wesleyan University Press, 2015), 64–67.

37. Horowitz, *Campus Life,* 167.

38. Babette Faehmel, *College Women in the Nuclear Age: Cultural Literacy and Female Identity, 1940–1960* (New Brunswick, NJ: Rutgers University Press, 2012), 180.

39. Deborah Elizabeth Whaley, *Disciplining Women: Alpha Kappa Alpha, Black Counterpublics, and the Cultural Politics of Black Sororities* (New York: State University of New York Press, 2010), 3–5. See also Walter M. Kimbrough, *Black Greek 101: The Culture, Customs, and Challenges of Black Fraternities and Sororities* (Madison, WI: Farleigh Dickinson University Press, 2000); Paula Giddings, *In Search of Sisterhood: Delta Sigma Theta and the Challenge of the Black Sorority Movement* (New York: William Morrow, 1988); Marjorie Parker, *Alpha Kappa Alpha through the Years, 1908–1988* (Chicago: Mobium, 1990).

40. See Robert Cohen and Reginald E. Zelnik, eds., *The Free Speech Movement: Reflections on Berkeley in the 1960s* (Berkeley: University of California Press, 2002), 119. See also Irwin Unger and Debbi Unger, eds., *The Times They Were A'Changin: A Sixties Reader* (New York: Three Rivers, 1998).

41. Mario Savio, quoted in Robert S. Cohen, *Freedom's Orator: Mario Savio and the Radical Legacy of the 1960s* (Oxford: Oxford University Press, 2009), 192.

42. See Richard Flacks and Nelson Lichtenstein, *The Port Huron Statement: Sources and Legacies of the New Left's Founding Manifesto* (Philadelphia: University of Pennsylvania Press, 2015).

43. Horowtiz, *Campus Life,* 232.

44. Martha Biondi, *The Black Revolution on Campus* (Berkeley: University of California Press, 2012). For an example in the Midwest, see Joy Ann Williamson, *Black Power on Campus: The University of Illinois, 1965–1975* (Urbana: University of Illinois Press, 2003).

45. These were the most famous student killings, but of course there were others, such as the student deaths resulting from law enforcement actions at South Carolina State University in 1968 and North Carolina Agricultural and Technical

State University in 1969. See I. H. Rogers, *The Black Campus Movement: Black Students and the Racial Reconstitution of Higher Education, 1965–1972* (New York: Palgrave Macmillan, 2012).

CHAPTER 5. THINKING FOR ONESELF BY LEARNING FROM OTHERS

1. Helen Lefkowitz Horowitz, *Campus Life: Undergraduate Cultures from the End of the 18th Century to the Present* (New York: Knopf, 1987), chap. 11.

2. The numbers grew to the point that about half of high school graduates enrolled in college, with much more significant increases among women. See *National Center for Education Statistics*, https://nces.ed.gov/programs/digest/d07/tables/dt07_191.asp.

3. On training and entanglement, see Kari Weil, *Thinking Animals: Why Animal Studies Now?* (New York: Columbia University Press, 2012), 58–59, 147–49.

4. Horace Mann, "Mr. Mann's Seventh Annual Report: Education in Europe," *Common School Journal* 6 (1844): 72.

5. Mark Seidenberg, *Language at the Speed of Sight: How We Read, Why So Many Can't and What We Can Do about It* (New York: Basic Books, 2018), 90, 113.

6. See John McWhorter, "We Know How to Teach Kids to Read," *New York Times*, September 3, 2021; Mark Seidenberg, *Language at the Speed of Sight*.

7. Elizabeth Green, "Building a Better Teacher," *New York Times Magazine*, March 7, 2010, https://www.nytimes.com/2010/03/07/magazine/07Teachers-t.html. See also her *Building a Better Teacher: How Teaching Works (and How to Teach It to Everyone)* (New York: Norton, 2014), 8–11, 94–97.

8. José Antonio Bowen, *Thinking Change: How to Develop Independent Thinkers Using Relationships, Resilience and Reflection* (Baltimore, MD: Johns Hopkins University Press, 2021).

9. Horowitz, *Campus Life*, 250.

10. Allan Bloom, *The Closing of the American Mind: How Higher Education Has Failed Democracy and Impoverished the Souls of Today's Students* (New York: Simon and Schuster, 1987), 51.

11. See Martha Nussbaum, "Undemocratic Vistas," *New York Review of Books*, November 5, 1987.

12. Allan Bloom, "Our Listless Universities," *National Review*, December 10, 1982, reposted at https://www.nationalreview.com/2006/09/our-listless-universities-williumrex/. See also Bloom, *The Closing of the American Mind*.

13. Menand is quoted in Andrew Ferguson, "The Book That Drove Them Crazy," *Weekly Standard*, April 9, 2012. The essay was adapted for the afterword of the twenty-fifth anniversary publication of *Closing* and can also be accessed at

https://www.washingtonexaminer.com/weekly-standard/the-book-that-drove-them-crazy.

14. Roger Kimball, *The Long March: How the Cultural Revolution of the 1960s Changed America* (New York: Encounter Books, 2001), 5.

15. Roger Kimball, "Tenured Radicals: A Postscript," *New Criterion*, January 1991, https://newcriterion.com/issues/1991/1/aoetenured-radicalsa-a-postscript.

16. A key theme of her *Campus Life*. See especially chap. 11, "The Nerds Take Revenge."

17. Kimball, "Tenured Radicals."

18. The core of what colleges and universities were assigning or requiring students to read was remarkably stable. Although there were a few newcomers to the list of required texts, Sophocles, Plato, and Aristotle were usually among the most often listed. Martin Luther King's *Letter from a Birmingham Jail* did make many lists around the country. In Columbia University's Core Program, one starts with Plato and Aristotle and ends with contemporary texts (in the final couple of weeks). There are fewer than a handful of women authors over the thirty-nine weeks.

19. William Deresiewicz, "Don't Send Your Kids to the Ivy League," *New Republic*, July 21, 2014; and Deresiewicz, *Excellent Sheep: The Miseducation of the American Elite and the Way to a Meaningful Life* (New York: Free Press, 2015). On Bloom and Deresiewicz, see Chad Wellmon and Paul Reitter, "Melancholy Mandarins: Bloom, Weber and Moral Education," *Hedgehog Review* 19, no. 3 (Fall 2018), https://chadwellmon.com/2018/02/24/melancholy-mandarins-bloom-weber-and-moral-education. In a subsequent work on political correctness, Deresiewicz moves closer to Bloom: "We Aren't Raising Adults. We Are Breeding Very Excellent Sheep," *Common Sense*, May 2022, https://www.commonsense.news/p/we-arent-raising-adults-we-are-breeding?s=r.

20. Michael Crow of Arizona State University is the higher-education leader who has done the most to call attention to this pattern and offer an alternative to it. See his (with William B. Dabars) *Designing the New American University* (Baltimore, MD: Johns Hopkins University Press, 2015).

21. Anthony Abraham Jack, *The Privileged Poor: How Elite Colleges Are Failing Disadvantaged Students* (Cambridge, MA: Harvard University Press, 2019), 23.

22. See Tina Wildhagen, " 'Not Your Typical Student': The Social Construction of the 'First-Generation' College Student," *Qualitative Sociology* 38 (2015): 285–303; Rachel Gable, *The Hidden Curriculum: First Generation Students at Legacy Universities* (Princeton, NJ: Princeton University Press, 2021).

23. Higher Education Act, *U.S. Department of Education*, https://www2.ed.gov/about/offices/list/ope/trio/triohea.pdf. See also Rochelle Sharpe, "Are You First Gen? Depends on Who's Asking," *New York Times*, November 3, 2017, https://www.nytimes.com/2017/11/03/education/edlife/first-generation-college-admissions.html?_r=0.

24. Robert K. Toutkoushian, Robert A. Stollberg, and Kelly A. Slaton, "Talking 'bout My Generation: Defining 'First-Generation College Students' in Higher Education Research," *Teachers College Record* 120, no. 4 (2018): 1–38, https://www.tcrecord.org, ID Number: 22042. From the conference presentation of the paper: "The focus on first-generation college students follows from the belief that these students on average face particular hardships that constrain their educational attainment." https://www.insidehighered.com/sites/default/server_files/files/Talking%20Bout%20My%20Generation%20Fall%202015%20ASHE.pdf.

25. See Raj Chetty's social mobility scorecards, many of which are collected at *Opportunity Insights,* https://opportunityinsights.org/education/.

26. Michael Sandel, *The Tyranny of Merit: What's Become of the Common Good?* (New York: Farrar, Straus and Giroux, 2020), 177.

27. Ibid., 60.

28. Richard Reeves, *Dream Hoarders: How the American Upper Middle Class Is Leaving Everyone Else in the Dust, Why That Is a Problem, and What to Do about It* (Washington, DC: Brookings Institute Press, 2017), 11, 100.

29. Terry Heick, "The Difference between Learners and Students," *Edutopia,* 2013, https://www.edutopia.org/blog/difference-between-learners-and-students-terry-heick.

30. Saga Briggs, "The Difference between Skilled Learners and Good Students," at *informED,* April 19, 2015, https://www.opencolleges.edu.au/informed/features/the-difference-between-skilled-learners-and-good-students/.

31. Patricia A. Alexander, "A+ Students/C– Learners: Education's Report Card," *Psychology Today,* February 24, 2015, https://www.psychologytoday.com/us/blog/psyched/201502/studentsc-learners-education-s-report-card.

32. Kathleen McClaskey, "Learner vs Student: Who Do You Want in Your Classroom?" *Make Learning Personal,* September 30, 2018, https://kathleenmcclaskey.com/2018/09/30/learner-vs-student/.

33. See "Active Learning Increases Student Performance in Science, Engineering, and Mathematics," *PNAS,* June 10, 2014, 8410–15. See also Cathy N. Davidson and Christina Katopodis, *The New College Classroom* (Cambridge, MA: Harvard University Press, 2022), 29–38.

34. Beth McMurite, "Why the Science of Teaching Is Often Ignored," *Chronicle of Higher Education,* January 2022, https://www.chronicle.com/article/why-the-science-of-teaching-is-often-ignored.

35. Cottom's work is described in Cathy Davidson, *The New Education: How to Revolutionize the University to Prepare for a World in Flux* (New York: Basic Books, 2017), 130. See also Tressie McMillan Cottom, *Lower Ed: The Troubling Rise of For-Profit Colleges in the New Economy* (New York: New Press, 2017).

36. Anthony Kronman, *The Assault on American Excellence* (New York: Free Press, 2019).

---

37. Roosevelt Montás, *Rescuing Socrates: How the Great Books Changed My Life and What They Can Do for a New Generation* (Princeton, NJ: Princeton University Press, 2021), 3, 12, 217. See also Gayle Greene, *Immeasurable Outcomes: Teaching Shakespeare in the Age of the Algorithm* (Baltimore, MD: Johns Hopkins University Press, 2023).

38. John Dewey, *Democracy and Education: An Introduction to the Philosophy of Education* (New York: Free Press, 1916). On Freire, see his *Pedagogy of the Oppressed* (New York: Bloomsbury, 2014). On Tagore, see Amiya Chakravarty, ed., *A Tagore Reader* (Boston: Beacon, 1961). See, for example, Martha C. Nussbaum, "Education and Democratic Citizenship: Capabilities and Quality Education," *Journal of Human Development* 7, no. 3 (2006): 385–95, doi:10.1080/146498806 00815974. See also her *Not for Profit: Why Democracy Needs the Humanities* (Princeton, NJ: Princeton University Press, 2010), especially chap. 4.

39. See the Foundation for Critical Thinking website: https://www.critical thinking.org/.

40. I borrow the phrase "critical feeling" from Rolf Reber, *Critical Feeling: How to Use Feelings Strategically* (Cambridge: Cambridge University Press, 2016). In the paragraphs that follow I draw on my "A Focus on Critical Feeling," *Inside Higher Ed*, March 18, 2021, https://www.insidehighered.com/views/2021/03/18/colleges-should-teach-critical-feeling-well-critical-thinking-opinion.

41. Mark Edmundson, "Teach What You Love," *American Scholar*, Autumn 2020, https://theamericanscholar.org/teach-what-you-love/.

42. See Paula Marantz Cohen, *Of Human Kindness: What Shakespeare Teaches Us about Empathy* (New Haven, CT: Yale University Press, 2021); Eddie S. Glaude Jr., *Begin Again: James Baldwin's America and Its Urgent Lessons for Our Own* (New York: Random House, 2020).

43. See Rita Felski, *The Limits of Critique* (Chicago: University of Chicago Press, 2015); Felski, *Critique and Post-Critique*, ed. Elizabeth S. Anker and Rita Felski (Durham, NC: Duke University Press, 2017); and Eboo Patel, *We Need to Build: Field Notes for Diverse Democracy* (Boston: Beacon, 2022).

44. See Friedrich Nietzsche, *Schopenhauer as Educator (1876)*, in *Untimely Meditations*, ed. Daniel Breazeale (Cambridge: Cambridge University Press, 1997); and also his 1872 lectures collected as *Anti-Education: On the Future of Our Educational Institutions* (New York: NYRB, 2015), ed. Paul Reitter and Chad Wellmon. On John Baldessari's pedagogy, see Jacquelyn Ardam, "On Not Teaching Art: Baldessari, Pedagogy and Conceptualism, *ASAP* 3, no. 1 (2018): 143–71; and Deborah Solomon, "John Baldessari: An Artist in a Class by Himself," *New York Times*, January 7, 2020, https://www.nytimes.com/2020/01/07/arts/design/john-baldessari-art.html.

45. William James, "On a Certain Blindness in Human Beings," in *The Writings of William James: A Comprehensive Edition*, ed. John J. McDermott (Chicago: University of Chicago Press, 1977), 634.

46. I've developed a historical account of pragmatic liberal education in *Beyond the University: Why Liberal Education Matters* (New Haven, CT: Yale University Press, 2014).

47. Martha C. Nussbaum, *Frontiers of Justice: Disability, Nationality, Species Membership* (Cambridge, MA: Harvard University Press, 2006).

48. Frank Bruni, *Where You Go Is Not Who You'll Be: An Antidote to the College Admissions Mania* (New York: Grand Central, 2015), 113. See also Jeffrey Selingo, *Who Gets In and Why: A Year Inside College Admissions* (New York: Scribner, 2020).

INDEX

INDEX

INDEX

6; slavery and, 71–77. *See also*
independence
Free Speech Movement, 135
Freire, Paulo, 170
Friedan, Betty: The Feminine Mystique,
132
Fuller, Buckminster, 132

gamification, 167
Gates, Henry Louis, 72
geometry, 70
Germany: academic freedom in, 94–95, 97,
100–101; Du Bois in, 111, 114–15,
189n9; Enlightenment in, 93, 95;
university culture in, 92–97
Givens, Jarvis R., 186n42
grammar, 70
Greek life organizations. *See* fraternities;
sororities
Green, Elizabeth, 146

habit, 81
Hall, G. Stanley, 144
Hanawalt, Barbara, 48, 50, 53
harmony, 15, 17
Hart, James Morgan, 98–103, 104, 108,
188n30
Harvard University, 111–12, 115, 161
Hayes, Rutherford B., 113–14
hazing, 69–70, 127
Hevel, Michael, 125, 128
hierarchies: apprenticeships and, 45,
52–53, 61; childhood learning of, 45,
51; fraternities and, 127–28;
meritocracy and, 155–56; political
movements and, 136–37; slavery and,
72
Higher Education Act of 1965, 160–64
historical continuity, 15
historically black colleges and universities
(HBCUs), 110

Horowitz, Helen, 122, 148, 152, 190n17
Howard University, 133
Howe, Irving, 131
humanism, 67, 95
Humboldt, Wilhelm von, 92–97, 105,
187n19; "On the Internal and
External Organization of the
Higher Scientific Institutions in
Berlin," 93
Hume, David, 72

immigrant students, 129
independence: agency and, 71; apprenticeships and, 46–51, 53, 55–56, 60–61,
71; economic, 45, 55, 66, 71, 76,
116, 118; freedom as, 4, 6; in
Humboldtian universities, 95;
individualism vs., 50–51; language
use and, 143; religious education and,
65–66; of women, 89–90. *See also*
freedom
individualism, 50–51, 132
Industrial Revolution, 56
in loco parentis, 55

Jack, Anthony Abraham, 159–60
Jackson State University, 139, 141
Jacobs, Harriet: Incidents in the Life of a
Slave Girl, 76
Jacobs Free School (Virginia), 76
James, William, 112, 173
Jansenism, 81–82
Jefferson, Thomas, 103–4, 123
Jesus, 3, 9, 38–44, 179
Jewish students, 127, 130
Ji Huanzi, 15
John the Baptist, 40
Johns Hopkins University, 156
Judaism, 38–39
Judas (biblical), 39, 42–43
justice, 32

199

INDEX

Kant, Immanuel: on classical education, 80;
definition of enlightenment, 4, 86, 92,
95, 149; on dissemination of
knowledge, 84; on enlightenment as
process, 92, 169–70, 179; on freedom
to question and reason, 79, 92;
influence on Du Bois, 112; influence
on German universities, 93;
Rousseau's influence on, 88; "What
Is Enlightenment?" 78, 80, 96, 100,
102
Kent State University, 139, 141
Kimball, Roger, 151, 152
King, Martin Luther: Letter from a
Birmingham Jail, 193n18
Knight, Louise, 119
Kronman, Anthony, 168

Laslett, Peter, 182n1
lateral learning, 125–26
Latin language, 58, 62–63, 68–69, 80–81
Lewis, David Levering, 109, 112, 114
Li (rites and rituals), 16–17
liberal arts education, 70, 109
literacy, 62–65, 73–75, 143–46
Locke, John, 81, 83, 152; Treatise on
Education, 67
low-income students, 159–64
loyalty, 21, 32–33, 38
Luther, Martin, 64–65

machine learning, 8
Mann, Horace, 144
Marcuse, Herbert, 132
Marxism, 152
mathematics, 79, 80, 146
Matthew (biblical), 39, 40–42
McAllester, David P., 132
McClaskey, Kathleen, 166
McWhorter, John, 145
Menand, Louis, 150

meritocracy, 155–56, 159–64
Milton, John: Paradise Lost, 82
Montás, Roosevelt, 168–69; Rescuing
Socrates, 169
moral virtues, 49, 52, 61
Morrill Act of 1890, 110
Morrison, Toni, 172
Mosley, Eleanor, 56
Mount Holyoke College, 122
multiculturalism, 152
music, 70

Napoleon Bonaparte, 93
Native American students, 139
Neo-Confucianism, 13
neoliberalism, 154–55
Nietzsche, Friedrich, 173
nihilism, 150
Nixon, Richard, 139–40
North Carolina Agricultural and Technical
State University, 191n45
Nussbaum, Martha, 176

Occom, Samson, 74–75
opportunity hoarding, 163–64
overconfidence, 33–34
Ovid: Metamorphoses, 63

Paul (biblical), 39, 43–44
PBL (project-based learning), 166–67, 169
Pell Grants, 161
Peloponnesian War (431–404 BCE), 24, 32
Peter (biblical), 39–40
Peters, Phillis Wheatley, 73–74, 185n38
Pharisees, 41
philosophy, 36–37, 86
piety, 33
pit schools, 76
Plato, 24, 25, 29–31, 182n28, 193n18;
Apology, 31, 36; Euthyphro, 33–34;
Republic, 31–32, 34, 171

200

INDEX

INDEX